Demo-Lib-Public

By:
Chris A. Tovmasian

Table of Contents

Introduction - A Divided Marketplace of Political Promises

A Nation at a Crossroads

America stands at a pivotal moment, its political landscape fractured, and its citizens polarized. The air crackles with tension, a sense of impending demolition hanging heavy. This "Demolibpublic," as we shall call it, is defined by a profound sense of division, distrust, and disillusionment with the very mechanisms that are supposed to guide the nation.

At the heart of this disarray lie three major players: the Democratic, Republican, and Liberal parties. Like competing titans in a grand marketplace, they vie for hearts and minds, each peddling their wares - ideologies, platforms, visions for the future. Yet, amidst the cacophony of promises and soundbites, a nagging question arises: are they truly offering different products, or merely the same packaged in distinct boxes with varying labels?

The Salesmen of Ideology

Imagine, for a moment, that these three parties are not political entities, but rival salesmen. Each takes to the stage, extolling the virtues of their product, promising prosperity, security, and a brighter tomorrow. The Democrats, perhaps, paint their product as one of compassion, championing social justice and economic equality. The Republicans, in contrast, might boast of its efficiency, touting fiscal responsibility and individual liberty. And the Liberals, standing slightly apart, present themselves as the purveyors of progress, advocating for innovation and environmental stewardship.

But as we listen closer, the similarities begin to emerge. The Democrats' promise of inclusivity might echo the Republicans' emphasis on opportunity. The Republicans' call for self-reliance may find resonance in the Liberals' pursuit of individual empowerment. All three, under the surface, might offer variations on the same themes: security, freedom, and a better life for all.

Beyond the Labels: Unmasking the Reality
This is not to say that differences do not exist. Each party boasts its own unique history, philosophical underpinnings, and policy priorities. The Democrats tend to prioritize social welfare programs and government intervention, while Republicans generally favor free-market solutions and limited government interference. Liberals, meanwhile, often champion individual rights, environmental protection, and social reform.

Yet, it is crucial to remember that these labels are not monolithic; they encompass a spectrum of viewpoints and internal factions. Democrats debate the extent of government involvement, Republicans grapple with the balance between individual liberty and collective responsibility, and Liberals navigate the complexities of social progress and economic security.

Demo-lib-public: A Call for Informed Engagement
The current state of American politics, however, presents a concerning trend. The emphasis on partisan loyalty and ideological purity often overshadows the search for common ground and constructive dialogue. The marketplace of political promises becomes a battleground, where facts are weaponized, opponents demonized, and compromise deemed a sign of weakness.

This "Demo-lib-public" threatens the very foundations of a healthy democracy. It impedes progress, fosters distrust, and hinders the nation's ability to confront its most pressing challenges.

Thus, the purpose of this book is not to simply chronicle the divisions or endorse any specific ideology. Rather, it seeks to illuminate the complex landscape of American politics, offering a factual and balanced analysis of the three major players. We will delve into their histories, dissect their platforms, and examine the impact of their policies on the nation's social, economic, and environmental well-being. Through this journey, we hope to empower readers to become informed and engaged citizens. By understanding the nuances of the political landscape, critically evaluating the promises presented, and seeking common ground amidst the differences, we can rebuild our "Demo-lib-public" into a space of constructive dialogue, collaborative problem-solving, and a shared vision for the future.

Part 1: The Three Parties

Chapter 1: From Jeffersonian Roots to Modern Strides: The American Democratic Party's Enduring Journey

The Democratic Party, the elder statesman of American politics, boasts a rich and complex history, etched with triumphs and tribulations, bold ideals and controversial decisions. This chapter delves into the party's captivating journey, from its Jeffersonian origins to its contemporary struggles, offering a nuanced perspective on its evolution, successes, and challenges.

1. Seeds of Democracy: Jeffersonian Ideals and Democratic Beginnings

The Democratic Party's roots trace back to Thomas Jefferson and his Democratic-Republican Party, champions of limited government, agrarian interests, and individual liberty. This Jeffersonian legacy, emphasizing states' rights, a decentralized government, and opposition to a powerful federal bureaucracy, formed the bedrock of early Democratic Party ideology.

Jefferson's philosophy was deeply rooted in the belief that a government closest to the people was most effective. He advocated for states' rights, arguing that local governance should prevail over a centralized federal system. This was in stark contrast to the Federalist Party at the time, which supported a strong central government. Jefferson's emphasis on decentralized government was a response to fears of tyranny and despotism, echoing the sentiments that fueled the American Revolution.

His political thought also emphasized an agrarian society, where farming and rural values were seen as the backbone of the nation. Jefferson believed that an agrarian society would support the virtues of hard work, self-reliance, and a connection to the land, which were essential for maintaining a democratic republic. This agrarian ideal stood in opposition to the rapid industrialization and urbanization that were beginning to take shape.

Additionally, Jefferson was a proponent of individual liberty. He held that personal freedoms were fundamental to a thriving democracy. His commitment to these principles is exemplified in his authorship of the Declaration of Independence, which asserts the unalienable rights of life, liberty, and the pursuit of happiness. This commitment extended to his opposition to a powerful federal bureaucracy, which he feared could infringe upon individual rights and freedoms.

The Jeffersonian legacy shaped the early ideology of the Democratic Party, influencing its policies and political stance. The party championed the rights of states, upheld the importance of an agrarian economy, and stood against the expansion of federal power. These principles resonated with many Americans, particularly those who were wary of centralized authority and valued personal freedoms.

Over time, the Democratic Party evolved, adapting to the changing social, economic, and political landscape of America. However, the seeds of democracy planted by Jefferson's ideals continued to influence the party's direction and policies. His vision of a government by the people, for the people, and of the people, remains a cornerstone of democratic governance and the pursuit of liberty and justice for all.

2. The Rise of Jacksonian Populism: A New Chapter for Democracy

The transformative period in American politics marked by the presidency of Andrew Jackson. His election in 1828 represented a significant shift in the political landscape, signaling the rise of Jacksonian Democracy, a movement that profoundly reshaped the Democratic Party and the nation's democratic ideals.

Jackson's populist approach was groundbreaking for its time. He appealed directly to white working-class men, a demographic that had previously felt marginalized in the political process. His campaign and subsequent victory were seen as a triumph for the common man over the established political elites, reflecting a deep-seated desire for more inclusive representation in government.

One of the key features of Jacksonian Democracy was the expansion of suffrage. Prior to this era, voting rights were typically limited to property-owning white males. Jackson's policies and political influence contributed to the dismantling of these restrictions, thereby broadening the electorate to include a larger segment of the white male population. This expansion of suffrage was a significant step toward a more democratic system, although it notably excluded women and people of color.

Jackson's presidency also prioritized westward expansion, which was a central theme of American policy during this period. This expansionist vision not only shaped the physical landscape of the United States but also had profound implications for the nation's political and social dynamics. The push towards the west, while contributing to the growth of the nation, also led to the controversial and tragic displacement of Native American tribes.

In terms of domestic policy, Jacksonian Democracy focused on infrastructure development. This emphasis on building roads, canals, and other public works was seen as essential for the nation's economic growth and the integration of its vast territories. These projects facilitated trade and communication, fostering a more interconnected and prosperous nation. Jackson's approach to politics was characterized by a straightforward, no-nonsense style that resonated with many Americans. He portrayed himself as a champion of the common man, standing against corrupt elites and entrenched interests. This persona helped solidify the Democratic Party's identity as the party of the people, committed to representing the interests and aspirations of the average American.

3. Civil War and Beyond: Defining Lines and Shifting Landscapes

The Civil War era marked a pivotal moment in the history of the Democratic Party, fundamentally reshaping its principles and political stance. The party's alignment with the Confederacy and support for states' rights, particularly in terms of slavery, led to a severe blow to its national influence following the Union's victory. This period of decline was further exacerbated by the Republican Party's dominance in the post-war Reconstruction era, a time characterized by significant efforts to rebuild the South and integrate freed slaves into American society.

During Reconstruction, the Democratic Party, particularly in the South, vehemently opposed the Republican-led initiatives that aimed to protect the civil and voting rights of African Americans. The establishment of Jim Crow laws, which enforced racial segregation and suppressed Black voting rights, was a direct result of the Democratic stronghold in the Southern states. These laws remained in effect for nearly a century, symbolizing the party's resistance to civil rights reforms.

As the 19th century drew to a close, the Democratic Party began to experience internal divisions. The split between its conservative wing, which maintained traditional views, and the more progressive members advocating for expanded government roles in ensuring social justice, marked the beginning of a significant ideological shift. The advocacy of leaders like William Jennings Bryan for a larger government role in social justice laid the groundwork for the party's later transformation during the Progressive Era. This period saw the Democrats begin to move away from their agrarian, conservative roots towards advocating for worker protections and social welfare programs, reflecting a growing alignment with urban, working-class Americans.

The ideological shift became more pronounced with the advent of Franklin D. Roosevelt and the New Deal in the 1930s. The New Deal represented a radical change in the role of the federal government in American life, introducing extensive social welfare programs, regulations for financial markets, and support for labor unions. This era solidified the Democratic Party's image as the champion of the working class, the underprivileged, and minorities. However, this transformation also deepened the rift within the party, particularly between the Southern Democrats and the more progressive Northern wing.

The post-Civil War transformation of the Democratic Party was not just a change in policy but also a reflection of the shifting social and economic landscapes in America. As the country moved from an agrarian society to an industrialized nation, the party's policies and priorities evolved to address the needs and challenges of a changing nation.

4. 20th Century and Beyond: Highs and Lows of a Century in Power

The 20th century witnessed the Democratic Party reaching new heights and facing significant challenges. Under the leadership of Franklin D. Roosevelt, the New Deal era established the Democrats as the party of economic intervention and social safety nets, reflecting a significant departure from its earlier stances. The New Deal's emphasis on social welfare, worker protections, and government intervention in the economy attracted a broad coalition of supporters, including labor unions, urban voters, and minority groups.

However, the party's ascendancy was not without its challenges. The Democratic Party's historical base in the segregationist South became a point of contention as the party began to embrace civil rights. The Civil Rights Movement of the 1960s, championed by Democratic Presidents John F. Kennedy and Lyndon B. Johnson, marked a significant turning point. The passage of landmark legislation like the Civil Rights Act of 1964 and the Voting Rights Act of 1965 was instrumental in advancing civil rights but also led to a political realignment, particularly in the South.

The Southern Democrats, known as "Dixiecrats," began to defect to the Republican Party, attracted by its opposition to the expansion of federal power and its stance on social issues. This shift was accelerated by the Republican Party's "Southern strategy," which sought to gain the support of disaffected white voters in the South. The strategy was successful, leading to a transformation in the political landscape of the South, which went from being a Democratic stronghold to a Republican-dominated region.

Despite these challenges, the Democratic Party continued to evolve, particularly in its stance on social issues.

5. Modern-Day Democratic Party: Strengths, Weaknesses, and Unfolding Future

In the contemporary political landscape, the Democratic Party embodies a diverse coalition, reflecting the complex and multifaceted nature of modern American society. The party's base includes environmentalists, feminists, civil rights advocates, and urban professionals, representing a wide range of interests and concerns. This diversity is both a strength and a challenge, shaping the party's policies and strategies.

Strengths

1. Advocacy for Progressive Policies: The party champions progressive stances on various social issues, including healthcare, LGBTQ+ rights, and climate change. This appeal to progressive values resonates with a significant portion of the electorate, particularly younger voters and urban populations.

2. Support for Social and Economic Equality: Democrats have consistently advocated for policies that support social and economic equality. This includes backing social welfare programs like Medicaid and food stamps and endorsing progressive taxation to fund these initiatives.

3. Emphasis on Civil Rights: The party has a long-standing commitment to the civil rights of minorities, advocating for policies that promote equality and justice. This commitment has earned the party the loyalty of various minority groups.

4. Environmental Focus: With growing concerns about climate change and environmental degradation, the party's strong stance on environmental protection aligns with the priorities of many Americans, particularly those who are environmentally conscious.

Weaknesses

1. Internal Divisions: One of the party's most significant challenges is the internal division between its moderate and progressive wings. This division often leads to conflicts over policy directions and can hinder the party's ability to present a unified front.

2. Difficulty Connecting with Rural Voter: The party has struggled to connect with rural voters, who often feel that their interests and lifestyles are not adequately represented by the Democratic platform. This has led to a geographical divide in the party's support base.

3. Navigating Economic Inequality and Political Polarization: The rise of economic inequality and increased political polarization pose significant challenges for the party. Balancing the interests of various economic groups while addressing the widening wealth gap is a complex task.

4. Globalization and Labor: Reconciling the party's historical pro-labor stance with the realities of globalization remains a contentious issue. The party must navigate the impacts of global economic trends on American workers while maintaining its commitment to labor rights.

Unfolding Future
Looking forward, the Democratic Party faces the task of navigating these strengths and weaknesses in a rapidly changing political landscape. The party's ability to adapt to evolving societal values, economic realities, and demographic shifts will be crucial in determining its future success. Balancing the diverse interests within its coalition, while addressing the challenges of political polarization and economic inequality, will be key to maintaining its relevance and effectiveness as a major political force in the United States.

Highlights and Failures: A Legacy of Progress and Controversy

The Democratic Party's historical journey is marked by significant achievements and notable controversies, reflecting the evolving nature of American politics and societal values.

Highlights of the Democratic Party

Expansion of Social Security: Initiated under President Franklin D. Roosevelt as part of the New Deal, the Social Security Act of 1935 is one of the Democratic Party's most significant achievements. It provided a safety net for the elderly, the unemployed, and others through federal benefits and marked a pivotal moment in American social welfare policy.

Civil Rights Act and Voting Rights Act: The Civil Rights Act of 1964 and the Voting Rights Act of 1965, both signed into law by Democratic President Lyndon B. Johnson, were landmark pieces of legislation that profoundly changed American society. These acts outlawed segregation and discriminatory voting practices, respectively, and played a crucial role in advancing civil rights in the United States.

Affordable Care Act (ACA): Enacted in 2010 under President Barack Obama, the ACA, commonly known as Obamacare, represented a significant overhaul of the U.S. healthcare system. It aimed to reduce the cost of health care and increase the quality and affordability of health insurance, expanding healthcare coverage to millions of uninsured Americans.

Failures and Controversies
Support for Slavery and Segregationist Policies: In its early years, the Democratic Party supported slavery, with many Democrats vehemently opposing abolition. Post-Civil War, the party was associated with enforcing segregationist policies, particularly in the Southern states, reflecting a stance that contradicts its later commitment to civil rights.
Foreign Policy Interventions: The Democratic Party has been involved in several controversial foreign policy decisions. For example, the Vietnam War escalated under Democratic Presidents John F. Kennedy and Lyndon B. Johnson, leading to widespread protest and criticism. Other foreign interventions, such as those in the Middle East, have also sparked debate and controversy over the party's foreign policy choices.

Pros and Cons: Defining the Party's Identity in the 21st Century

The Democratic Party, facing the 21st century's complexities, grapples with defining its identity amidst a dynamic political landscape. A key strength lies in its unwavering commitment to social justice, championing civil rights, gender equality, and LGBTQ+ rights, which resonates with a younger and more diverse electorate. Additionally, its stance on environmental protection and policies aimed at providing economic opportunities for all have bolstered its appeal among those concerned with sustainability and social equity. However, the party is not without its challenges. Internal divisions, spanning a spectrum from moderate to progressive ideologies, often create friction that hinders unified policy-making and presents a fragmented front. This fragmentation is further exacerbated by difficulties in connecting with certain demographics, particularly rural, working-class, and some minority groups, which is crucial for building a comprehensive electoral coalition.

The Road Ahead: A Party in Transition and a Nation Divided

As the Democratic Party stands at a crossroads, it confronts several pressing challenges. Navigating the internal fissures between its progressive and moderate wings is paramount to maintaining unity and effectiveness in policy implementation. Moreover, in an era marked by economic anxieties and rapid information flow, the party faces the daunting task of crafting policies that resonate with a broad base while staying relevant and responsive to emerging issues. The divisive nature of modern politics adds another layer of complexity, making bipartisan cooperation and appealing to independents and moderates increasingly challenging.

Yet, despite these challenges, the party's dedication to progress and its diverse coalition offer a beacon of hope. The rich tapestry of perspectives and ideas stemming from its varied base provides a unique advantage. Furthermore, the party's ability to adapt and evolve in response to new challenges and shifting public sentiments stands as a testament to its potential for growth and increased relevance. As the nation finds itself divided on many fronts, the Democratic Party's journey is emblematic of the broader quest for balance and adaptation in an ever-changing political and social environment.

Chapter 2: From Anti-Slavery to Big Business: The Republican Party's Transformation

The Republican Party, often characterized by its elephant emblem, embodies a fascinating metamorphosis in American political history. From its fiery anti-slavery origins to its modern focus on fiscal conservatism and business interests, the party's journey is a tale of idealism, conflict, and adaptation.

1. *Roots in Righteous Anger: The Anti-Slavery Movement and the Birth of the GOP*

The origins of the Republican Party are deeply intertwined with the anti-slavery movement, a pivotal force in American politics during the mid-19th century. The party's formation was a direct response to the pro-slavery sentiments that were prevalent among the existing political establishments, particularly the Whig Party and the Democrats. During the 1850s, a sense of disillusionment grew among those who opposed slavery. This group primarily consisted of former Whigs, along with a significant number of antislavery activists, who were increasingly frustrated with the lack of a strong political voice against slavery.

The burgeoning Republican Party found its roots in a righteous anger against the institution of slavery, which was seen not only as a moral abomination but also a threat to free labor and the values of the American Republic. The Missouri Compromise's failure, which attempted to balance the power between slave and free states, and the violent events of "Bleeding Kansas," where pro-slavery and anti-slavery settlers clashed, served as catalysts that galvanized the anti-slavery movement. These events highlighted the urgent need for a political solution to the slavery issue and underscored the limitations and failures of existing policies and political parties in addressing this growing national crisis.

The creation of the Republican Party was, therefore, more than just the formation of a new political entity; it was a moment of reckoning for the United States. It represented a collective stand against the spread of slavery into new territories and states, a stand that was as much about moral conviction as it was about shaping the future political and economic landscape of the nation. The Republican Party's dedication to halting the expansion of slavery was not only a key aspect of its identity but also a defining factor in the lead-up to the American Civil War. The party's emergence from the anti-slavery movement marked a significant turning point in American political history, laying the groundwork for a profound shift in the nation's approach to slavery and its eventual abolition.

2. *The Lincoln Legacy: Uniting a Nation, Defining a Party*

Abraham Lincoln's ascendancy to the presidency in 1860 heralded a significant turning point in American history, both for the nation and the Republican Party. His leadership during one of the country's most tumultuous eras, the Civil War, was instrumental in not only preserving the Union but also in defining the identity and ethos of the Republican Party. Lincoln's presidency coincided with a period of profound crisis and division within the United States. The secession of the Southern states and the outbreak of the Civil War posed an existential threat to the Union. Lincoln's response to this crisis, characterized by a blend of steadfast determination and strategic acumen, played a critical role in keeping the Northern states united against the Confederacy.

One of the most defining acts of Lincoln's presidency was the Emancipation Proclamation. Although this decree, which declared the freedom of all slaves in Confederate-held territory, was primarily a war measure, it had profound symbolic and practical implications. It marked a decisive shift in the war's aim, transforming it from a battle to preserve the Union into a moral crusade against slavery. This act significantly bolstered the Republican Party's standing as the champion of freedom and equality, aligning it firmly against the institution of slavery.

Lincoln's approach to abolition and the Civil War was complex and nuanced. He navigated a delicate balance between his moral opposition to slavery and the political and practical considerations of the time. His primary objective was the preservation of the Union, but he increasingly recognized that achieving this goal was intertwined with addressing the issue of slavery. This nuanced approach helped in rallying a broad coalition of support, crucial for the war effort and for the Republican Party's growing influence.

Lincoln's legacy in uniting a deeply divided nation and his unwavering commitment to the abolition of slavery became defining pillars of the Republican Party's identity. His presidency established the GOP as a party committed to fundamental human rights and the principles of liberty and equality. This legacy continued to shape the party's policies and philosophies long after his assassination, cementing his place as one of the most influential figures in American political history.

3. Reconstruction's Bittersweet Harvest: Challenges and Controversies

Reconstruction, the tumultuous period following the American Civil War, was marked by a series of significant challenges and controversies that shaped the nation's path towards healing and integration. For the Republican Party, which was at the forefront of this era, Reconstruction presented an unprecedented opportunity to reshape the South and integrate millions of newly freed slaves into American society. However, the task was fraught with difficulties and resistance, leading to a period characterized by both notable achievements and profound setbacks.
The primary goal of Reconstruction was to reintegrate the Southern states that had seceded and to define the new status of the freed slaves. Republicans, under the leadership of figures like Ulysses S. Grant, embarked on ambitious programs aimed at rebuilding the devastated Southern infrastructure and economy, as well as promoting civil rights for African Americans. This included the establishment of institutions like the Freedmen's Bureau and the passage of the 13th, 14th, and 15th Amendments, which abolished slavery, granted citizenship to all born in the U.S., and protected voting rights regardless of race, respectively.

However, the process was met with significant resistance. The political landscape of the era was complex, marred by presidential assassinations, the rise of the so-called Bourbon Democrats in the South who sought to maintain the old social order, and the emergence of groups like the Ku Klux Klan that violently opposed the integration and empowerment of African Americans. These factors created a volatile environment, where progress in civil rights and infrastructure redevelopment was consistently undermined by political battles, economic inequities, and entrenched racial tensions. One of the most significant challenges was the integration of freed slaves into Southern society. Despite the legal abolishment of slavery, African Americans faced widespread discrimination, disenfranchisement, and violence. The Black Codes, enacted by Southern states, were designed to restrict the freedoms of African Americans and ensure a labor force subservient to white interests, revealing the deep-seated racial prejudices that persisted even after the abolition of slavery. Economically, the South struggled to transition from its reliance on slave labor to a more diversified economy. The destruction wrought by the war, combined with the lack of investment in the region, led to widespread poverty and economic stagnation. This was further complicated by the political instability of the era, with frequent changes in policies and leadership as the nation grappled with the assassination of President Lincoln and the subsequent presidential administrations.

Reconstruction, therefore, was a bittersweet harvest for the Republicans and the nation. While it laid the groundwork for significant civil rights advancements and attempted to rebuild and modernize the South, it also unveiled the deep-rooted challenges that would continue to plague the United States for decades to come. The era was a complex mix of hope and disillusionment, progress and regression, highlighting the enduring struggle of a nation striving to reconcile its ideals with the realities of its divided past.

4. Shifting Tides: From Civil Rights to Big Business

As the United States transitioned out of the Reconstruction era, the Republican Party underwent a significant evolution, reflecting the changing priorities and dynamics of the country. The late 19th and early 20th centuries were characterized by rapid industrialization and economic growth, which ushered in a new phase for the party, marked by a shift in focus from civil rights to economic and business interests.
During Reconstruction, the Republican Party was primarily known for its strong stance on civil rights and its efforts to rebuild and integrate the South. However, as the nation's economy started to grow and industrialize, the party's priorities began to evolve. The rise of big business and industrialism brought about a new set of concerns and interests that began to dominate the political agenda. The Republican Party responded to these changes by increasingly advocating for policies that favored business and industry. One of the key aspects of this transformation was the party's support for business-friendly policies. This included advocating for high tariffs to protect American industries from foreign competition, promoting policies that favored industrial growth, and supporting the interests of the burgeoning class of industrialists and entrepreneurs. These policies were seen as essential for fostering economic growth and maintaining America's competitiveness in the rapidly industrializing world.
Alongside this economic shift, the party also began to embrace the concept of limited government intervention in the economy. This philosophy was grounded in the belief that a less regulated market would encourage innovation, entrepreneurship, and economic expansion. The Republican Party's stance appealed to the growing class of industrialists and business owners, who saw government intervention as a potential hindrance to their enterprises.

While some members of the party continued to champion civil rights issues, these concerns became increasingly secondary to the party's economic agenda. This shift was partly a response to the political and social realities of the time, as the country grappled with the challenges of managing rapid economic growth and addressing the needs of an increasingly diverse and urbanized population.

As a result, the Republican Party began to attract a new base of support, drawing in wealthy industrialists, entrepreneurs, and members of the urban middle class. These groups were attracted to the party's pro-business stance and its commitment to policies that promoted economic growth and industry.

This transition marked a significant reorientation of the Republican Party's priorities, from its post-Civil War focus on civil rights and Reconstruction to a new emphasis on economic development, business interests, and limited government intervention. This shift in focus played a crucial role in shaping the party's identity and policies in the decades to follow, reflecting the changing tides of American politics and society in the face of industrialization and economic transformation.

5. *Modern-Day GOP: A Balancing Act of Conservatism and Progress*

In the contemporary political landscape, the Republican Party presents itself as a complex amalgamation of diverse ideologies and perspectives, balancing between its conservative roots and the more moderate factions within its ranks. This balancing act is a defining characteristic of the modern-day GOP, reflecting the party's evolution and its response to the changing dynamics of American politics and society.

The core of the Republican Party's platform is grounded in principles of conservatism, which include a strong emphasis on fiscal responsibility, the advocacy of free markets, and a commitment to social conservatism. Fiscal responsibility, a long-standing tenet of the party, involves advocating for reduced government spending, lower taxes, and minimizing national debt. The party's economic policies are rooted in the belief that free markets and minimal government intervention are key drivers of economic growth and prosperity.

Social conservatism, another pillar of the party, manifests in stances on various social issues that often place the GOP at odds with the Democratic Party. This includes opposition to abortion, advocating for gun rights, and a generally cautious approach to environmental regulation. These positions resonate with a significant portion of the party's base, which values traditional social norms and individual liberties as defined by their interpretation of the Constitution.

However, the modern GOP also contends with internal debates that reflect the diversity of its membership and the complexity of current political issues. Immigration is one such issue, where the party grapples with reconciling the need for border security and law enforcement with the economic benefits of immigration and humanitarian considerations. Healthcare is another area of contention, with debates centered around the extent of government involvement in healthcare and the best approach to ensuring access while maintaining quality and controlling costs.

The party's approach to climate change exemplifies the balancing act between traditional conservatism and a response to evolving public concerns and scientific consensus. While traditionally skeptical of significant government intervention in environmental matters, there is a growing recognition within the party of the need to address climate issues, albeit with solutions that align with conservative principles, such as market-based mechanisms and technological innovation.

From Morality to Marketplaces: A Legacy of Change and Controversy

The Republican Party's journey through American history is a narrative of profound transformation, marked by its foundational commitments and evolving ideologies. This legacy, much like a double-edged sword, embodies both celebrated achievements and contentious shifts that have continually shaped and reshaped the party's identity and impact on American politics.

In its inception, the Republican Party was grounded in principles of anti-slavery and union preservation. Its formation was a direct response to the moral crisis of slavery and the imminent threat it posed to the American Union. The party's early years were defined by a staunch commitment to ending slavery, as epitomized by Abraham Lincoln's presidency and the Union's victory in the Civil War. This period marked the GOP as a champion of moral righteousness and a defender of the Union, engraining these principles as core elements of its legacy.

However, as the nation evolved, so did the Republican Party. The post-Civil War era saw a gradual but significant shift in the party's focus. Moving away from its early emphasis on civil rights and Reconstruction, the GOP began to align more closely with the interests of burgeoning industrial and business sectors. This shift was driven by the rapid economic growth and industrialization of the late 19th and early 20th centuries. The party's advocacy for business-friendly policies, high tariffs, and limited government intervention in the economy reflected its adaptation to the changing economic landscape.

This transition towards economic conservatism and business interests marked a new phase in the Republican Party's evolution. While these policies fostered economic growth and appealed to a growing class of industrialists and urban middle classes, they also led to controversies and debates, particularly regarding the balance between corporate interests and worker rights, environmental conservation, and economic inequality. Simultaneously, the party's stance on social issues began to reflect a conservative ethos, particularly in the latter half of the 20th century. Stances on issues such as abortion, gun rights, and environmental regulation solidified the GOP's identity as a bastion of social conservatism. While these positions resonated with many Americans, they also fueled debates and controversies, particularly as the nation grappled with issues of personal liberties, social justice, and environmental sustainability.

The Republican Party's legacy, therefore, is one of significant change and enduring controversy. From its moral crusade against slavery to its embrace of free-market capitalism and social conservatism, the party's history reflects the dynamic and often contentious nature of American politics. This legacy is not only a testament to the party's adaptability and influence but also a reminder of the ongoing debates and challenges that continue to define American political discourse.

Pros and Cons: Defining the Party's Identity in the 21st Century.

Pros

Commitment to Fiscal Responsibility: One of the Republican Party's key strengths is its strong advocacy for fiscal conservatism. This includes policies aimed at reducing government spending, lowering taxes, and minimizing national debt, appealing to voters who prioritize economic efficiency and a smaller government footprint in economic affairs.

Advocacy of Free Markets: The party's staunch support for free market principles is a cornerstone of its identity. This stance, emphasizing minimal government intervention in the economy, appeals to entrepreneurs, businesses, and those who believe in the power of the market to drive innovation, economic growth, and job creation.

Focus on National Security: The GOP is traditionally viewed as strong on issues of national security and defense. Its policies often emphasize a robust military, a firm stance against terrorism, and assertive foreign policy, resonating with voters who prioritize safety and global leadership.

Cons

Internal Divisions: The Republican Party faces challenges due to ideological divisions within its ranks, particularly between its traditional conservative base and more moderate or libertarian factions. These internal disagreements can hinder consensus and unified action on policy matters.

Struggles to Connect with Certain Demographics: The GOP has historically struggled to connect with certain demographic groups, including younger voters, racial and ethnic minorities, and in some cases, women. This challenge limits the party's ability to build a broad and diverse electoral coalition.

Rigid Stance on Social Issues: The party's often rigid stance on various social issues, such as abortion, LGBTQ+ rights, and immigration, can be polarizing. While these positions align with the views of their conservative base, they can also alienate more moderate voters and those who prioritize social justice and inclusivity.

The Road Ahead: Bridging Divides and Charting a New Course

Looking towards the future, the Republican Party stands at a critical juncture where it must navigate a path that balances its core principles with the increasingly diverse and evolving needs of the American electorate. This challenge involves not only reaffirming the party's traditional stances but also adapting and responding to emerging societal issues in a way that broadens its appeal and addresses the concerns of a wider range of voters.

One of the key areas where the GOP faces a need for balance is healthcare. The debate over healthcare in the United States has been a contentious one, with opinions within the party ranging from complete repeal of the Affordable Care Act to advocating for more moderate reforms. Going forward, the party will need to find a consensus that upholds its principles of free-market solutions and personal responsibility while also addressing the public's growing concerns about accessibility, affordability, and quality of healthcare.

Climate change represents another significant area where the Republican Party is challenged to chart a new course. While traditionally skeptical of aggressive environmental regulations and climate policies, there is an increasing recognition, especially among younger party members, of the need to address environmental issues. The party could explore market-based solutions and technological innovations that align with its economic principles while effectively tackling the challenges posed by climate change.

Social justice is an additional domain where the GOP could seek common ground. The party's traditional base has often been at odds with social justice movements. However, addressing issues related to racial inequality, criminal justice reform, and equal rights in a manner that resonates with its principles of individual liberty and justice can help the party connect with a broader electorate, including younger voters and minority groups.

The road ahead for the Republican Party involves a complex balancing act. It must maintain its identity and core principles while also evolving to meet the changing demands of a diverse and dynamic society. Bridging divides within the party and among the broader public on these key issues will be crucial for the GOP's future relevance and success. This endeavor will require thoughtful engagement, innovative policy solutions, and a willingness to adapt to the shifting landscape of American politics and society.

Chapter 3: Liberalism's Enduring Journey: From Philosophical Roots to Modern Debates

Liberalism, a philosophy as vast as a continent and as varied as its inhabitants, has shaped the Western world and deeply influenced American politics. Let's embark on a voyage through its intellectual history, tracing its evolution, exploring its impact on the American landscape, and delving into its diverse strands.

1. Seeds of Liberty: The Philosophical Wellspring

The philosophical underpinnings of liberalism have their roots deeply entrenched in the ideas and theories of prominent 17th and 18th-century thinkers, particularly John Locke and Montesquieu. These philosophers, through their groundbreaking work, laid the groundwork for what would eventually be recognized as classical liberalism, a doctrine that has significantly influenced modern political and social thought.

John Locke, often regarded as the father of liberalism, introduced concepts that have become fundamental to liberal thought. His theories emphasized the importance of individual rights and the idea that government power should be derived from the consent of the governed. Locke's assertion that individuals have natural rights to life, liberty, and property was revolutionary. It challenged the prevailing notions of absolute monarchy and divine right, proposing instead that governments are formed to protect these inherent rights and that their legitimacy comes from the consent of those they govern.

Another cornerstone of Locke's philosophy was the concept of the social contract, the idea that individuals collectively agree to form a society and a government to protect their rights but retain the power to change or dismantle that government should it fail to serve its intended purpose. This idea profoundly influenced the development of democratic governance and constitutionalism.

Baron de Montesquieu, another key figure in the development of liberal thought, contributed significantly with his ideas on the separation of powers within a government. His work, "The Spirit of the Laws," articulated the idea that political authority should be divided into separate branches—legislative, executive, and judicial—to prevent the concentration of power and the potential for tyranny. This concept of checks and balances became a fundamental principle in the design of many modern democratic governments, most notably in the United States Constitution.

The ideas championed by Locke, Montesquieu, and other Enlightenment philosophers like Voltaire and Rousseau formed the philosophical bedrock of classical liberalism. They advocated for a political and social order that respected individual freedoms, promoted limited government, and upheld the rule of law. These principles stood in stark contrast to the prevailing autocratic and often oppressive political structures of their time.

Classical liberalism, with its emphasis on individual liberty, rationality, and equal rights, set the stage for various modern political ideologies and movements. It inspired revolutions, such as the American and French Revolutions, and laid the foundation for contemporary democratic societies. The legacy of these Enlightenment thinkers is evident in the ongoing global pursuit of liberty, justice, and democratic governance.

2. Crossing the Atlantic: Liberalism Flourishes in America

The transplantation and flourishing of liberal ideas in the American colonies represented a pivotal moment in the history of political thought, particularly as these ideas found a unique and fertile ground for implementation. The American colonists, grappling with what they perceived as the tyranny of British rule, found a profound resonance with the principles of classical liberalism, which advocated for self-determination, individual rights, and limited government. This confluence of circumstances and ideas set the stage for a revolutionary transformation, both in thought and governance.

The American Revolution, fueled by these liberal principles, became more than just a struggle for independence from British rule; it was a crucible for the fusion of classical liberalism with the principles of republicanism. This fusion formed the backbone of the emerging American political identity and the foundation of the United States government. Key among these liberal principles was the idea of checks and balances, a concept championed by Montesquieu. The American founders, acutely aware of the dangers of concentrated power, incorporated this principle into the Constitution, creating a system of government where power was distributed across three branches — legislative, executive, and judicial. This structure was designed to prevent any one branch from becoming too powerful, ensuring a balance that would protect individual liberties and prevent tyranny. Another cornerstone of the American system was the emphasis on individual liberties. Influenced by the writings of John Locke and others, the Founders believed strongly in protecting the rights of individuals. This belief was enshrined in the Bill of Rights, the first ten amendments to the Constitution, which guaranteed fundamental rights such as freedom of speech, religion, and assembly, and protections against governmental abuse of power.

Representative democracy was also a key aspect of the new American system. The idea that governments should be based on the consent of the governed, a principle central to liberal thought, was integral to the American experiment. The Founders created a system where representatives, elected by the people, would make decisions on their behalf, ensuring that the government reflected the will of its citizens.

The American Revolution and the subsequent establishment of the United States can thus be seen as a significant moment in the history of liberal thought. It was here that the theoretical concepts of classical liberalism were put into practice on an unprecedented scale. The new American system of government, with its emphasis on checks and balances, individual liberties, and representative democracy, became a model of liberal governance and a beacon of inspiration for liberal movements and democracies around the world.

3. Branching Out: The Diversification of Liberal Thought

As the 19th century progressed, liberal thought, rooted in the
ideas of Enlightenment philosophers, began to diversify and
branch out into various schools of thought, each offering its
own interpretation and emphasis on the core principles of
liberalism. This diversification represented a natural evolution
of liberal ideas in response to the changing social, economic,
and political landscapes of the time.

One significant branch that emerged was classical liberalism,
which continued to develop and refine the ideas of early
liberal thinkers like John Locke. The classical liberal tradition
strongly emphasized minimal government intervention in
both economic and personal affairs, advocating for free
markets and individual liberties. This branch found strong
advocates in thinkers like Adam Smith and David Ricardo.
Adam Smith, in particular, with his seminal work "The Wealth
of Nations," laid the foundations for modern economic theory.
He argued for the "invisible hand" of the market, suggesting
that free-market competition would lead to wealth creation
and overall societal benefit. David Ricardo furthered these
economic ideas, especially with his theories on comparative
advantage in international trade.

In contrast to the economic focus of classical liberalism, social
liberalism emerged as a branch concerned with addressing
issues of social justice and inequality. This school of thought
recognized that while political and economic freedoms were
essential, they were insufficient in ensuring true liberty and
well-being for all members of society. Social liberals argued
for a more active role of the government in addressing social
and economic disparities.

John Stuart Mill was a pivotal figure in social liberalism. His work, particularly "On Liberty" and "The Subjection of Women," advocated for individual freedom and equal rights but also recognized the necessity of societal intervention to protect the vulnerable and ensure a level playing field. Mill's ideas about liberty were not just about freedom from government intervention but also about creating the conditions in which individuals could truly thrive.

Karl Marx, although more often associated with socialism and communism, also contributed to the diversification of liberal thought, particularly in his critique of capitalist societies and his emphasis on addressing economic inequalities. While Marx's ideas would eventually branch off into a distinctly different ideological direction, his early work contributed to the broader discourse on social justice and economic equality within the liberal tradition.

This diversification of liberal thought in the 19th century reflected the complexities of a rapidly industrializing and changing world. It demonstrated the flexibility and adaptability of liberal ideas, as they were reinterpreted and applied to new social and economic challenges. The branching out of liberalism into classical and social strands represented an ongoing dialogue about the role of the individual, the market, and the state in promoting freedom, equality, and prosperity.

4. American Soil Nourishes New Growth: American Liberalism Takes Shape

The unique political and social landscape of America provided fertile ground for the growth and evolution of liberal thought, intertwining both classical and social liberal ideals. This intertwining was particularly evident during the Progressive Era, a period of significant reform and change in the United States spanning the late 19th and early 20th centuries.

On the one hand, the Progressive Era saw a surge in social liberalism, with reformers drawing on the ideas of social justice, equality, and government intervention to protect the rights and welfare of individuals. These reformers campaigned vigorously for a range of causes that echoed the core tenets of social liberalism. One of the most notable achievements of this period was the advancement of women's suffrage, culminating in the ratification of the 19th Amendment in 1920, which granted women the right to vote. This was a significant milestone in the pursuit of gender equality and a reflection of the growing recognition of individual rights and liberties.

Labor rights and protections also received substantial attention during this period. Progressive reformers advocated for better working conditions, reasonable working hours, and the establishment of child labor laws. These efforts were driven by a recognition of the inequities and exploitations prevalent in the rapidly industrializing economy of the time and a belief in the need for government intervention to ensure fair and humane labor practices.

In addition to social reforms, the Progressive Era was also characterized by efforts to address economic inequalities and abuses of power. This was where the influence of classical liberalism, with its emphasis on free markets and individual liberties, intersected with a growing recognition of the need for regulation. The era saw the implementation of antitrust laws, such as the Sherman Antitrust Act, designed to curb the power of monopolies and promote fair competition. These laws represented a nuanced approach to economic policy, acknowledging the benefits of free markets while also recognizing the need for government intervention to prevent abuses and ensure a level playing field.

The American approach to liberalism during the Progressive Era thus represented a blend of classical and social liberal ideals. It maintained a commitment to individual rights and free markets, as advocated by classical liberalism, while also embracing the social liberal emphasis on equality, social justice, and the role of government in addressing social and economic issues. This synthesis shaped the nation's political landscape and laid the groundwork for many of the social and economic policies that would define American society in the following decades.

5. *The 20th Century's Crucible: New Deal Liberalism and Beyond*

The Great Depression of the 1930s served as a critical turning point for liberalism in the United States, challenging the prevailing liberal doctrines and leading to a significant reorientation of liberal thought. The economic and social crises brought on by the Depression called for urgent and innovative responses, which were embodied in President Franklin D. Roosevelt's New Deal. This suite of programs and policies marked a decisive shift towards a more interventionist role for the government in economic and social matters, laying the groundwork for what came to be known as "New Deal liberalism" or "modern liberalism."

Prior to the Great Depression, classical liberalism, with its emphasis on limited government intervention and laissez-faire economics, had a significant influence on American policy. However, the severity of the Depression, characterized by widespread unemployment, bank failures, and economic stagnation, exposed the limitations of these classical principles in addressing such profound economic and social challenges.

In response, FDR's New Deal represented a dramatic shift in the role of the federal government. It introduced a range of programs aimed at providing immediate relief to those suffering from the Depression, promoting economic recovery, and implementing reforms to prevent future economic crises. Key components of the New Deal included the Social Security Act, which established a system of old-age pensions and unemployment insurance; the Works Progress Administration (WPA), which created millions of jobs through public works projects; and the Federal Deposit Insurance Corporation (FDIC), which aimed to restore trust in the banking system.

The New Deal also encompassed significant regulatory reforms, such as the Securities and Exchange Commission (SEC) to regulate the stock market and prevent abuses like those that contributed to the 1929 crash. These reforms reflected a belief in the need for government oversight to ensure fairness and stability in the economy.

This evolution towards New Deal liberalism marked a reconciliation of classical liberal ideals of individual liberty and free markets with a recognition of the government's responsibility to ensure economic stability and social welfare. It acknowledged that without certain social safety nets and economic regulations, the free market alone could not guarantee widespread prosperity and security.

The legacy of New Deal liberalism extended far beyond the Roosevelt era, shaping American political and social policies for decades. It laid the foundation for subsequent social welfare programs and became a cornerstone of the Democratic Party's platform. Moreover, it redefined the American public's expectations of the role of government, with an increased acceptance of federal involvement in economic and social affairs as a means to promote the general welfare and protect individual rights.

New Deal liberalism thus represents a critical phase in the evolution of liberal thought in America, illustrating the flexibility and adaptability of liberalism in responding to the changing needs and challenges of society.

6. Contemporary Divergences: Debates and Challenges in the 21st Century

Today, liberalism continues to be a dynamic and evolving political philosophy, adapting to the complexities and challenges of modern society. The globalized world, marked by rapid technological advancements, environmental concerns, and changing social dynamics, has spurred new debates within the liberal tradition, leading to divergences in how its core principles are interpreted and applied.
One of the central themes in contemporary liberal thought is the response to globalization. The increasing interconnectedness of the world's economies, cultures, and political systems has raised questions about the role of government in regulating international trade, immigration, and global governance. While some liberals advocate for free trade and open borders, emphasizing the benefits of global integration, others express concerns about the impact of globalization on local industries, workers' rights, and national sovereignty. This tension reflects the ongoing debate within liberalism about balancing the benefits of a globalized world with the need to protect local communities and economies. Technological advancements, particularly in the digital realm, have also presented new challenges for liberalism. Issues such as data privacy, cybersecurity, and the impact of social media on democracy are at the forefront of these challenges. Liberals grapple with how to protect individual freedoms and privacy in an increasingly digital world while ensuring that technology is used responsibly and ethically.

Environmental concerns, especially climate change, represent another significant area of debate within contemporary liberalism. There is a growing recognition of the need for collective action and government intervention to address environmental issues. Progressive liberals often advocate for strong regulatory measures to protect the environment, viewing climate change as a global crisis that requires a coordinated response. In contrast, other liberals emphasize market-based solutions and individual responsibility, arguing that innovation and private sector involvement are key to addressing environmental challenges.

The role of government in social and economic affairs continues to be a central theme in liberal thought. Some liberals argue for a more progressive approach, emphasizing the need for government action to address social justice issues, economic inequality, and healthcare. This perspective often involves advocating for expanded social welfare programs, progressive taxation, and government intervention to correct market failures and ensure equal opportunities.

Conversely, there are those who prioritize individual liberty and limited government intervention, arguing that personal freedom and market forces are the best drivers of prosperity and social progress. This viewpoint emphasizes the importance of individual choice, free markets, and minimal government involvement in personal and economic matters.

These divergences within contemporary liberalism reflect the ongoing evolution of the ideology in response to new societal challenges. The debates and discussions within liberal thought are indicative of its adaptability and relevance in addressing the complex issues of the 21st century. As liberalism continues to evolve, it remains a vital and influential force in shaping political and social policies around the world.

Strengths and Weaknesses: A Nuanced View of Liberalism

Liberalism, as a political and philosophical ideology, offers a nuanced and multifaceted view of society, governance, and individual rights. Its strengths and weaknesses can be examined through the lens of its core principles and the practical implications of these principles in modern societies.

Strengths of Liberalism

Commitment to Individual Freedom: One of the key strengths of liberalism is its unwavering commitment to individual freedom, which includes the protection of civil liberties and personal autonomy. This focus ensures that individuals have the right to express themselves, pursue their interests, and live without undue interference from the state.

Advocacy for Equality: Liberalism champions equality before the law, advocating for equal rights and opportunities for all individuals, regardless of their background. This principle has been fundamental in promoting social progress, including movements for gender equality, racial equality, and LGBTQ+ rights.

Upholding the Rule of Law: The emphasis on the rule of law is another strength of liberalism, ensuring that laws are applied fairly and consistently. This principle protects individuals from arbitrary governance and is crucial for maintaining social order and justice.

System of Checks and Balances: Liberalism advocates for a system of governance with checks and balances, preventing any single branch of government from becoming too powerful. This system is crucial for protecting democratic values and preventing authoritarianism.

Fostering Tolerance and Diversity: Liberal societies tend to be more open and tolerant, embracing diversity in cultures, ideas, and beliefs. This environment encourages creativity, innovation, and a dynamic civil society.

Weaknesses of Liberalism

Potential Neglect of Social Justice: Critics argue that liberalism's focus on individual rights can sometimes overlook or insufficiently address issues of social justice and collective welfare. This gap can lead to disparities in areas like healthcare, education, and social services.

Exacerbation of Economic Inequality: While liberalism promotes free markets and economic freedoms, this can sometimes lead to increased economic inequality. The emphasis on market autonomy may result in insufficient regulation and oversight, allowing for wealth concentration and limited social mobility.

Challenges in Balancing Freedom and Regulation: Finding the right balance between individual freedoms and necessary government intervention can be challenging. Too little regulation may lead to social and economic issues, while too much can infringe on personal liberties.

Globalization and Sovereignty Concerns: In a globalized world, liberal principles like free trade and open borders can clash with concerns about national sovereignty and local economic interests, leading to complex debates on immigration, trade policies, and cultural identity.

Environmental Considerations: The liberal focus on industrial and economic growth has, at times, led to environmental neglect. Addressing climate change and environmental degradation requires a rethinking of how liberal principles align with sustainable practices.

In summary, while liberalism has been instrumental in promoting individual rights, equality, and democratic governance, it also faces challenges and criticisms, particularly in addressing social justice, economic inequality, and environmental sustainability. These strengths and weaknesses highlight the ongoing need for liberalism to adapt and evolve in response to contemporary societal needs and challenges.

The Road Ahead: Finding Common Ground in a Divided Landscape

In today's increasingly polarized and complex global landscape, liberalism faces the significant challenge of finding common ground while addressing the multifaceted concerns of the contemporary world. This challenge involves a nuanced balancing act between preserving individual liberty and upholding social responsibility. Liberal thought must navigate the delicate interplay between promoting economic freedom and ensuring environmental sustainability, recognizing that economic growth should not come at the expense of ecological health. As globalization continues to reshape societies, liberalism is tasked with reconciling the benefits of open borders and free trade with the imperatives of national sovereignty and equitable economic development.
Further, contemporary liberalism must adapt to the rapid technological advancements that define our era, addressing the implications for privacy, the nature of work, and the spread of misinformation. This adaptation requires a forward-looking approach that embraces innovation while guarding against its potential drawbacks, such as job displacement and threats to individual privacy. In addition, there is a pressing need to foster a culture of reasoned debate and factual discourse to counter the rising tide of misinformation and polarization.

Crucially, liberalism must evolve to ensure inclusivity and represent the diversity of modern societies. This evolution entails not only advocating for the rights and freedoms of all individuals but also actively working to dismantle systemic barriers and inequalities. By embracing a broader and more inclusive understanding of freedom, equality, and justice, liberalism can continue to be a relevant and potent force for progress and democratic governance. In sum, the road ahead for liberalism is one of continuous adaptation and thoughtful engagement with the challenges and opportunities presented by our ever-changing world.

Chapter 4: Navigating the Political Spectrum: A Comparative Analysis of Democrats, Republicans, and Libertarians

The American political landscape is a vibrant, and sometimes tumultuous, ecosystem populated by diverse ideologies vying for influence. Three major parties – Democrats, Republicans, and Libertarians – occupy distinct territories within this landscape, each with their own set of core values, platforms, and policy priorities. This chapter delves into a comparative analysis of these three political entities, illuminating their common threads and stark differences.

1. Core Ideologies and Values:

Democrats: Centered around social justice, equality, and environmental protection, Democrats generally favor government intervention to address social and economic inequities. They prioritize policies like universal healthcare, progressive taxation, and environmental regulations. Their core values include individual liberty, social responsibility, and environmental stewardship.

Republicans: Emphasizing individual liberty, fiscal responsibility, and national security, Republicans generally advocate for limited government intervention and free markets. They prioritize policies like tax cuts, deregulation, and a strong military. Their core values include individual independence, self-reliance, and traditional values.

Libertarians: Championing individual liberty above all else, Libertarians advocate for minimal government intervention in most aspects of life. They prioritize policies like personal liberty, free markets, and non-interventionism. Their core values include individual autonomy, limited government, and personal responsibility.

2. *Platforms and Policy Priorities:*

Democrats:
Social Policy: Focus on LGBTQ+ rights, abortion rights, gun control, and criminal justice reform.
Economic Policy: Advocate for income equality, minimum wage increases, and affordable healthcare.
Environmental Policy: Prioritize climate change action, renewable energy, and environmental protection.

Republicans:
Social Policy: Generally, oppose same-sex marriage, abortion, and gun control. Support traditional family values and religious freedom.
Economic Policy: Advocate for tax cuts, deregulation, and reduced government spending.
Environmental Policy: Often skeptical of climate change, prioritize economic growth over environmental regulations.

Libertarians:
Social Policy: Support individual liberty on most social issues, generally favor non-interference in personal choices.
Economic Policy: Advocate for free markets, minimal taxation, and privatization of government services.
Environmental Policy: Generally, support environmental protection, but often advocate for market-based solutions.

3. *Similarities and Overlapping Concerns:*

Despite their varied core ideologies, the Republican, Democratic, and Libertarian parties in the United States find commonality on several fronts. All three parties value the concept of individual liberty, albeit with different interpretations. This shared value underscores a fundamental belief in the importance of personal freedoms and rights within the American political landscape. Additionally, there is a consensus on the necessity of limiting government overreach, though the extent and areas where this is emphasized differ among the parties. Another area of agreement is the importance of maintaining a robust national defense, essential for the country's security and global standing.

When it comes to issues like education, healthcare, and infrastructure, all three parties recognize their importance but propose different methods and priorities for addressing them. These differences in approach reflect the diverse ideological underpinnings of each party but do not diminish the shared acknowledgment of these issues' significance in ensuring a prosperous and well-functioning society.

4. Stark Differences and Points of Contention:

The most pronounced differences among these parties lie in their stances on social issues, the role of government, and economic policies. Democrats and Republicans often find themselves at odds over issues such as abortion rights, gun control, LGBTQ+ rights, and climate change policies. Democrats tend to advocate for more protective legislation and government intervention in these areas, reflecting a broader interpretation of the government's role in safeguarding individual rights and addressing social issues. On the other hand, Republicans usually emphasize personal responsibility, individual choice, and limited government intervention, advocating for policies like tax cuts and deregulation.
The Libertarian Party stands distinct from both, with a core philosophy that centers on maximal individual liberty and minimal government interference. This philosophy translates into positions that often diverge significantly from those of both Democrats and Republicans, particularly in areas like drug legalization, foreign policy, and economic regulation.

Part 2: Political Theater and Landscape

Chapter 5: Partisanship in Action: Unmasking the Machinery of American Politics

The American political landscape is a whirlwind of ambition, strategy, and yes, sometimes, a dash of chicanery. But beneath the surface, a sophisticated machinery hums, driven by the powerful force of partisanship. In this chapter, we'll dissect the mechanisms that fuel campaigns, mobilize voters, and shape the very landscape of American elections.

1. Campaign Cash: The Fuel that Makes the Engine Roar

Money plays a pivotal role in the world of politics, serving as the lifeblood that keeps the political engine running. The flow of funds in politics is extensive and diverse, originating from a wide range of sources, including individual citizens and powerful special interest groups. Various fundraising mechanisms, such as campaign dinners, Political Action Committees (PACs), and Super PACs, inject millions of dollars into campaign coffers, powering the relentless pursuit of electoral victory. However, this substantial financial influence does not come without scrutiny and ethical considerations, leading to an ongoing debate about campaign finance reform within the political arena.

In the realm of campaign finance, concerns often center around the potential for undue influence. The influx of money into political campaigns can raise questions about whether the interests of wealthy donors or powerful organizations take precedence over the needs and desires of the general electorate. This concern underscores the importance of transparency and accountability in the handling of campaign funds.

A notable data point that highlights the scale of campaign spending is the staggering $14.4 billion that was poured into federal elections during the 2020 election cycle. This figure is indicative of the immense financial resources that are mobilized in the pursuit of political power and influence. Of particular note is the significant contribution of Super PACs, which alone provided over $1 billion in funding. These independent expenditure committees have the capacity to shape the political landscape through their financial contributions, further emphasizing the need for oversight and regulation in campaign finance.

A pertinent case study that illustrates the potential pitfalls of fundraising in politics is the 2016 Clinton Foundation controversy. This high-profile incident underscored the complex ethical considerations surrounding campaign financing. Questions were raised about potential conflicts of interest and the perception of undue influence stemming from donations to a charitable foundation associated with a prominent political figure. This case serves as a reminder of the importance of maintaining transparency, adhering to ethical standards, and addressing potential conflicts when it comes to campaign fundraising.

In conclusion, campaign finance is a crucial aspect of the political process, providing the necessary resources for campaigns to operate effectively. However, the significant financial power at play also gives rise to concerns about influence, transparency, and ethics. The substantial sums involved in political fundraising, as seen in the 2020 election cycle, underscore the need for ongoing scrutiny and reform efforts to ensure that the democratic process remains fair, accountable, and representative of the interests of all citizens.

The Narrative War Room:
Gone are the days of bullhorns and town squares; contemporary campaigns play out in a digital war room, where data analysts are generals and algorithms are the foot soldiers. The ability to craft a winning narrative, one that resonates with specific demographics and sways emotions, is the cornerstone of a successful campaign. It's an art form honed through meticulous research, deep understanding of voter psychology, and a healthy dose of creativity.

Microtargeting the Message:
Imagine firing an arrow that doesn't just hit the target but pierces its bullseye. Microtargeting allows campaigns to do just that. By leveraging vast datasets on voter demographics, online behavior, and even past voting records, campaigns can tailor their messages to specific groups with laser precision. Think single mothers receiving messages about affordable childcare, veterans hearing promises of enhanced healthcare, and young voters engaged through social media memes advocating for climate action. The 2020 study's finding that microtargeting swayed 300,000 votes underscores the power of this invisible sniper in the campaign arsenal.

The Weapon of Words: Crafting the Winning Narrative:
But beyond data points, lies the heart of the campaign: the
narrative. It's the overarching story that binds issues together,
connects with voters on an emotional level, and defines the
"why" behind the candidate's vision. Barack Obama's 2008
campaign perfectly illustrates the art of the persuasive
narrative. His message of "hope and change" resonated with a
nation weary of war and economic recession. It offered a
glimmer of possibility, a feeling of shared destiny, and a clear
contrast to the incumbent's policies. Obama's narrative wasn't
just a slogan; it was a movement, a call to arms that united
millions under a banner of optimism.

Beyond the Words: The Tools of Persuasion:
But words alone don't win elections. The narrative is
amplified through carefully crafted visuals, strategic media
placements, and targeted rallies. Imagine impactful campaign
ads mirroring Hollywood trailers, designed to evoke specific
emotions and trigger action. Picture meticulously planned
rallies, not just in battleground states but in unexpected swing
districts, designed to energize the base and create a sense of
momentum. Every detail, from the candidate's clothing to the
choice of music, is meticulously orchestrated to reinforce the
narrative and leave a lasting impression.

The Art of Attack: Taking Down the Opponent:
While crafting a compelling narrative is crucial, mastering the
art of attack is equally important. This doesn't mean resorting
to mudslinging; it's about exposing vulnerabilities,
highlighting inconsistencies, and portraying the opponent's
narrative as unrealistic or dangerous. Think fact-checking
debates in real-time, utilizing social media to counter
misinformation, and framing policy positions as detrimental
to specific voter groups. Remember, the goal isn't just to
dismantle the opponent's narrative; it's to solidify your own as
the credible and trustworthy alternative.

Mobilizing the Troops: From Clicks to Votes:
A winning campaign requires not just supporters, but active participants. Social media platforms become mobilization tools, where dedicated volunteers share content, organize events, and encourage voter registration. Think phone banks staffed by passionate supporters, text message campaigns reminding voters to cast their ballots, and online platforms connecting volunteers with specific tasks. The goal is to transform passive support into active engagement, ensuring that every click translates into a vote on election day. The battle for the hearts and minds of voters is waged on a complex battlefield, where data is the ammunition, the narrative is the weapon, and the human connection is the ultimate prize. Understanding the art of the pitch in modern campaigning is not just about understanding elections; it's about understanding how stories shape choices, how emotions influence decisions, and how the invisible threads of persuasion weave the fabric of democracy. So, the next time you see a campaign ad, listen for the narrative, dissect the message, and remember: this is not just a battle for votes; it's a battle for the soul of a nation, and the power of the pitch lies at the very heart of it.

3. The Foot Soldiers: Mobilizing the Masses

The success of any political campaign hinges not only on financial resources but also on the dedication and efforts of an army of volunteers and foot soldiers. These committed individuals play a pivotal role in campaigns by canvassing neighborhoods, tirelessly phone banking, and actively engaging with voters in their communities. Grassroots movements harness the power of social media and activism to drive voter turnout and shape political discourse, ensuring that democracy remains an active and participatory process rather than running on autopilot.

A significant data point that underscores the importance of grassroots mobilization is the remarkable voter turnout witnessed in the 2020 presidential election, reaching its highest level in over a century. This surge in voter participation can be partially attributed to the intensive efforts of grassroots organizers and volunteers who worked tirelessly to mobilize voters, particularly in key battleground states. Their dedication helped ensure that a record number of eligible voters exercised their right to participate in the democratic process.

A compelling case study that exemplifies the potency of grassroots activism is the Bernie Sanders' 2016 presidential campaign. This campaign was marked by its ability to galvanize a passionate volunteer base and ignite a social media movement. Sanders' grassroots supporters were instrumental in challenging the political status quo and advancing progressive policies. Their tireless efforts, both online and on the ground, played a pivotal role in shaping the political discourse of the election and amplifying key issues such as income inequality and healthcare reform.

The success of campaigns like Bernie Sanders' highlights the transformative potential of grassroots activism. It demonstrates that dedicated volunteers and grassroots organizers can mobilize a groundswell of support, particularly among younger and more progressive demographics. Grassroots movements have the capacity to challenge established political structures and foster political change by engaging directly with communities, sparking conversations, and mobilizing individuals who might otherwise be disengaged from the political process.

The human engine of mobilization, comprised of passionate volunteers and grassroots activists, is a driving force in shaping the outcomes of political campaigns. Their efforts, coupled with the use of social media and community engagement, have the potential to significantly impact voter turnout and influence the direction of political discourse. The example of the Bernie Sanders' campaign serves as a powerful testament to the ability of grassroots movements to challenge the status quo and bring about meaningful change in the political landscape.

4. Lines in the Sand: Gerrymandering's Uneven Playing Field

Gerrymandering, the practice of strategically manipulating electoral district boundaries, is a contentious and powerful tool in the arsenal of partisan politics. This practice involves redrawing electoral districts in a way that concentrates the voting power of one party's supporters while diluting the opposition's, effectively skewing the electoral playing field in favor of the party in control of the redistricting process. While gerrymandering has long been a subject of legal challenges and ethical concerns, it remains a prevalent reality in many states, distorting the electoral landscape and raising fundamental questions about the principles of fair representation in a democracy.

A notable data point that underscores the impact of gerrymandering is a 2018 study revealing that this practice resulted in at least 30 seats in the U.S. House of Representatives being awarded to the wrong party. This statistical finding highlights the direct consequences of gerrymandering on the composition of legislative bodies and the representation of the electorate. Such distortions in electoral outcomes can have far-reaching implications for policy decisions and the democratic process.

A pertinent case study that illustrates the detrimental effects of gerrymandering is the 2010 redistricting in North Carolina. This redistricting effort was subsequently found to be illegally gerrymandered, leading to significant disenfranchisement of voters and undermining the principles of democratic representation. In this case, partisan interests were prioritized over the fair and equitable representation of the state's diverse population. The subsequent legal battles and court rulings demonstrated the contentious nature of gerrymandering and the challenges in addressing it within the existing legal framework.

The practice of gerrymandering raises fundamental questions about the integrity of the electoral system and the bedrock principles of democracy. It challenges the idea that elections should reflect the will of the people and that every vote should carry equal weight. Gerrymandering also highlights the critical role of redistricting processes in shaping the political landscape, as it can enable the party in power to entrench its dominance and perpetuate a cycle of partisan advantage.

Gerrymandering remains a controversial and potent tool in American politics, with significant consequences for the representation of the electorate. The data and case study presented here emphasize the need for ongoing scrutiny, legal challenges, and reform efforts to address the challenges posed by this practice and ensure that the democratic principles of fair representation and equal participation are upheld in the electoral process.

5. The Incumbency Advantage: Power Once Acquired, Power Retained

The incumbency advantage is a well-documented phenomenon in politics, where once elected, politicians enjoy a range of built-in advantages that significantly boost their chances of retaining their positions. These advantages include access to government resources, high name recognition among constituents, and a track record of their performance in office. The combination of these factors makes incumbents formidable competitors in future elections.

One of the primary advantages of incumbency is access to government resources. Incumbent politicians have the ability to use the resources of their office, such as staff, funding, and facilities, to support their re-election campaigns. This access allows them to reach constituents more effectively and to maintain a visible presence in their districts or states.

Another crucial advantage is the high name recognition that incumbents enjoy. Through their time in office, incumbents become well-known figures in their communities or states. Voters are often more familiar with incumbent politicians, which can create a sense of trust or comfort among the electorate.

Additionally, incumbents have a track record in office that they can leverage during their campaigns. They can point to their accomplishments, legislative records, and constituent services as evidence of their effectiveness as representatives. This track record can be a persuasive factor for voters who may be hesitant to vote for an unknown challenger.

Incumbents also have the opportunity to build strong relationships with their constituents over time. Through town halls, constituent services, and regular communications, incumbents can establish connections with voters that may be challenging for challengers to replicate.

The incumbency advantage is further reinforced by the ability of incumbents to secure funding for their campaigns. They often have established donor networks and the ability to attract financial support from interest groups and political action committees (PACs). This financial advantage allows incumbents to run well-funded campaigns that can be difficult for challengers to match.

A significant data point that illustrates the power of incumbency is the high re-election rate for incumbents in the U.S. Congress. Since 1946, over 90% of House incumbents and over 80% of Senate incumbents who run for re-election have been successful. This statistic highlights the formidable challenge that challengers face when running against incumbents.

A case study that exemplifies the power of incumbency is Senator Susan Collins's 2020 re-election campaign in Maine. Despite facing a strong challenger and a highly competitive race, Senator Collins was able to secure victory. Her long tenure in office, high name recognition, and ability to attract campaign funding were critical factors in her successful re-election bid.

While the incumbency advantage can benefit individual politicians, it also raises concerns about accountability and competition in the political system. It can create a scenario where breaking into office as a newcomer becomes a daunting task, potentially discouraging qualified individuals from entering politics. Additionally, it can limit turnover in elected positions, which may have implications for the responsiveness of government to changing public needs and concerns.

In conclusion, the incumbency advantage is a powerful and persistent feature of American politics. It provides incumbents with access to resources, high name recognition, and a track record that significantly enhances their chances of re-election. While this advantage can benefit individual politicians, it also raises important questions about accountability, competition, and the overall health of the democratic process.

6. Beyond the Binary: Cracks in the System and Voices for Change

The dominance of the two-party system in American politics has faced challenges from various quarters. Third-party movements, independent candidates, and a growing chorus of discontent with the status quo have been pushing for new voices and perspectives within the political landscape. These forces advocate for diverse solutions, seek to break the two-party stranglehold on policy, and aim to make the political system more representative of the American people.

One notable data point that indicates a growing appetite for alternatives to the two major parties is the performance of third-party candidates in the 2020 election. These candidates collectively received a record 5.4% of the popular vote, suggesting that a significant portion of the electorate is open to considering alternatives to the Democratic and Republican parties. This data point underscores the potential for third-party and independent movements to gain traction and influence American politics.

A compelling case study that highlights the potential impact of third-party movements is the rise in popularity of the Green Party. The Green Party advocates for environmental sustainability, social justice, and progressive policies. While the party has not achieved widespread electoral success at the national level, it has garnered attention and support, particularly in local and state elections. The Green Party's presence and advocacy have forced major parties to address environmental and social justice issues, demonstrating the influence of third-party movements on the national agenda. Another case study that illustrates the potential of third-party movements is Bernie Sanders's independent presidential runs. Although Sanders ran as a Democrat in the 2016 and 2020 Democratic primaries, he identifies as an independent and has consistently championed progressive policies. His campaigns energized a substantial portion of the electorate and influenced the policy discourse within the Democratic Party. Sanders's campaigns showcased how independent and third-party candidates can shape the national conversation and compel major parties to address new issues and concerns. The push for alternatives to the two-party system is driven by a desire for greater representation and more diverse perspectives in American politics. Critics of the two-party system argue that it can lead to a lack of choice for voters and a limited range of policy options. By advocating for third-party movements and independent candidates, individuals and groups seek to expand the political spectrum and ensure that a wider array of voices are heard in the decision-making process.

In conclusion, while the two-party system remains dominant in American politics, there is a growing movement advocating for alternatives. Third-party movements, independent candidates, and discontent with the status quo are challenging the two-party stranglehold on policy and striving to make the political landscape more representative of the American people. The data point of increased support for third-party candidates and case studies like the Green Party and Bernie Sanders demonstrate the potential for these movements to influence the national agenda and force major parties to address new issues and concerns.

7. The Future of Partisanship: Can We Break the Wheel?

The future of partisanship in American politics raises important questions about how to overcome the limitations of the current system and build a more responsive and participatory democracy. Several potential paths forward have been proposed, each aimed at addressing the challenges posed by the existing political landscape.
One potential avenue for reform lies in campaign finance. Proposals for campaign finance reform include public funding of elections and stricter regulations on private contributions. Public funding of elections aims to reduce the influence of money in politics by providing candidates with public funds for their campaigns, thereby reducing their dependence on private donors. Stricter regulations on political spending seek to increase transparency, limit the influence of special interest groups, and level the playing field for candidates. Notably, public support for campaign finance reform remains high, with over 70% of Americans favoring stricter regulations on political spending, according to a data point.

Another pathway to reform involves structural changes to the electoral process. Ranked-choice voting is one such reform that has gained traction in some states. Ranked-choice voting allows voters to rank candidates in order of preference, and it eliminates the need for separate primary elections. This system encourages candidates to appeal to a broader range of voters and promotes compromise, as candidates seek to secure second-choice votes. States like Maine and Alaska have adopted ranked-choice voting, and they provide examples of how electoral reforms can incentivize candidates to focus on broader appeal and foster a more competitive political landscape.

Independent redistricting commissions are another structural reform aimed at reducing the power of the two-party duopoly. These commissions are tasked with drawing electoral district boundaries in a non-partisan manner, reducing the potential for gerrymandering and ensuring that districts are more representative of the population. Independent redistricting commissions aim to create fairer electoral maps and mitigate the impact of partisan manipulation in the redistricting process.

The pursuit of these reforms is driven by a desire to create a more responsive and inclusive democracy that better represents the diverse perspectives of the American people. Critics of the current system argue that it can lead to polarization, gridlock, and limited choices for voters. By advocating for campaign finance reform and structural changes to the electoral process, individuals and organizations seek to break the wheel of partisanship and foster a more competitive and representative political landscape.

The future of partisanship in American politics is a topic of ongoing debate and reform efforts. Campaign finance reform and structural changes like ranked-choice voting and independent redistricting commissions offer potential paths forward to create a more responsive and participatory democracy. Public support for these reforms underscores the desire for change and the recognition of the need to address the limitations of the current political system. Case studies of states like Maine and Alaska provide examples of how electoral reforms can incentivize candidates to focus on broader appeal and compromise, offering hope for a more competitive and inclusive political landscape in the future.

Conclusion: From the Grindstone to the Crossroads

Partisanship in American politics is a multifaceted and dynamic phenomenon, driven by a combination of factors including money, strategy, and the pursuit of power and influence. Understanding the mechanics and dynamics of partisanship is crucial for citizens to navigate the complex political landscape, hold elected officials accountable, and actively shape a future where democracy genuinely serves the interests of the people.

Partisanship often involves the allocation of significant financial resources, with campaign funding and contributions playing a central role. Political parties and candidates rely on fundraising efforts, including donations from individuals, corporations, and interest groups, to support their campaigns. The role of money in politics raises questions about the influence of donors and the potential for special interests to shape policy decisions.

Strategic considerations also drive partisanship, with parties and candidates employing various tactics to gain a competitive edge. This includes messaging strategies, voter outreach efforts, and campaign techniques aimed at mobilizing their base and winning over undecided voters. The strategic dimension of partisanship encompasses the use of data analytics, media advertising, and ground operations to secure electoral victories.

At its core, partisanship reflects the human desire for power and influence in the political arena. Elected officials, party leaders, and political operatives seek to advance their agendas and promote their preferred policies. The pursuit of power often involves coalition-building, negotiation, and compromise, as well as competition with rival parties and factions.

While partisanship is a fundamental aspect of democratic politics, the challenge lies in ensuring that it does not stifle diverse voices, manipulate the playing field, or impede progress. A healthy democracy should encourage robust debate, the representation of a wide range of perspectives, and responsive governance.

The question is not whether partisanship will always exist, as it is inherent to democratic systems, but whether it can be managed in a way that promotes the collective good. Through informed civic participation, critical thinking, and a sustained push for political reforms, citizens can strive to transform the grindstone of partisanship into a crossroads of progress. This vision entails reshaping the machinery of American politics to prioritize the broader interests of society over narrow party ambitions.

Achieving this transformation requires ongoing efforts to reduce the influence of money in politics, promote transparency and accountability, and implement electoral reforms that enhance competition and representation. It also entails fostering a culture of constructive political discourse and compromise, where elected officials prioritize the common good above partisan interests.

In conclusion, partisanship is a complex and enduring feature of American politics, but it is not insurmountable. By actively engaging in the political process, advocating for reform, and demanding accountability from elected officials, citizens can work towards a future where democracy serves the interests of the people and partisanship becomes a force for progress rather than division.

Chapter 6: Bipartisanship: A Bridge or a Broken Ladder?

In the political arena, where opposing colors clash and battle lines are drawn, a flicker of hope often emerges in the form of bipartisanship. This elusive ideal, where Republicans and Democrats join hands to forge common ground, promises compromise, progress, and solutions beyond the partisan divide. But is bipartisanship in today's climate a sturdy bridge over the political chasm, or a tattered ladder teetering on the brink of collapse?

A History of Shared Strides:

History provides valuable glimpses of the potential for bipartisan cooperation and the capacity of elected officials to work across party lines to achieve significant progress. Two notable examples illustrate the power of cooperation and compromise in advancing the interests of the American people.

The Civil Rights Act of 1964 stands as a beacon of equality and social justice in American history. This landmark legislation aimed to dismantle racial segregation and discrimination in various facets of American life. What makes this achievement remarkable is the bipartisan nature of its support. Republican Senator Everett Dirksen played a pivotal role in garnering support for the bill, working alongside Democratic President Lyndon B. Johnson. Their collaboration and leadership led to the passage of this historic legislation. The Civil Rights Act of 1964 remains a testament to the idea that when elected officials put aside partisan divisions and prioritize the common good, they can enact transformative change.

Another significant example of bipartisan cooperation is the effort to modernize Medicare in 1997. This initiative aimed to ensure access to healthcare for millions of seniors. It was a bipartisan effort that involved cooperation between Republican and Democratic lawmakers. The result was the Balanced Budget Act of 1997, which included provisions to improve and expand Medicare. This bipartisan achievement demonstrated that when elected officials come together to address pressing issues, they can make progress that benefits the American people.

These triumphs from the past serve as powerful reminders that progress can indeed blossom when compromise and cooperation outweigh partisanship. They highlight the potential for elected officials to work across party lines in pursuit of the greater good, even in the face of complex and contentious issues. These examples also underscore the importance of leadership and statesmanship in bridging divides and finding common ground.

While partisanship remains a significant challenge in American politics, history offers hope and inspiration for those who believe in the capacity of elected officials to rise above political divisions and work collaboratively to address the pressing issues of our time. The lessons from these historical moments serve as a call to action for today's leaders and citizens, encouraging them to prioritize cooperation and compromise in the pursuit of progress and a better future for all.

Case Study: The Infrastructure Investment and Jobs Act:

The passage of the Infrastructure Investment and Jobs Act in 2021 serves as a compelling case study of bipartisan cooperation and the ability of both parties to come together to address critical national priorities. This landmark legislation represents a glimmer of hope and a departure from the prevailing cynicism about partisan gridlock in American politics.

The Infrastructure Investment and Jobs Act is a significant and comprehensive investment in America's infrastructure, encompassing areas such as roads, bridges, broadband, and more. What makes this achievement remarkable is the bipartisan nature of its support. Lawmakers from both the Republican and Democratic parties worked together to draft and pass the bill, demonstrating their commitment to addressing the country's infrastructure needs.

The key factors that contributed to the success of this bipartisan effort include:

Shared Priorities: Both parties recognized the importance of infrastructure investment for the country's economic growth, competitiveness, and the well-being of its citizens. Infrastructure has long been a bipartisan issue, and there was a common understanding of the need for substantial upgrades and improvements.

Negotiation and Compromise: Lawmakers engaged in extensive negotiations and were willing to compromise on various aspects of the bill. This willingness to find middle ground and make concessions was instrumental in reaching a bipartisan agreement.

Broad Public Support: Infrastructure investment enjoys broad public support, and this was reflected in the willingness of lawmakers to prioritize the issue. Public demand for improvements to roads, bridges, and broadband access provided further motivation for bipartisan action.

Presidential Leadership: President Joe Biden played a crucial role in facilitating the negotiations and rallying support for the bill. His leadership and commitment to finding common ground were essential in bringing both parties to the table.

Recognition of Economic Benefits: Lawmakers recognized that the Infrastructure Investment and Jobs Act would have significant economic benefits, including job creation and increased economic productivity. This recognition incentivized bipartisan support.

The passage of this infrastructure bill demonstrates that collaboration and bipartisanship are possible, even on complex and substantial legislative initiatives. It serves as a positive example of what can be achieved when elected officials prioritize the needs of the nation over partisan divisions.

The Infrastructure Investment and Jobs Act is not only a substantial investment in physical infrastructure but also a symbol of the potential for bipartisan cooperation to address pressing national challenges. It offers hope that, in the face of significant issues, elected officials can come together to find solutions that benefit the American people and the country as a whole. This case study serves as an inspiring example for future efforts to bridge political divides and prioritize the common good.

The Cracks in the Bridge:

While bipartisanship has demonstrated its potential in certain areas, the bridge of bipartisanship also bears the scars of political conflict and division. Several contentious issues continue to ignite fierce partisan passions, making compromise on these topics challenging. Additionally, the influence of social media echo chambers and ideologically-driven news outlets has contributed to the deepening of political divides, further eroding the common ground essential for cooperation.

Some of the key challenges and cracks in the bridge of bipartisanship include:
Gun Control: The issue of gun control has long been a divisive and polarizing one in American politics. Deeply held beliefs and concerns on both sides of the debate make it difficult to find common ground and pass comprehensive gun control legislation.
Abortion: Abortion is another highly contentious issue that elicits strong emotions and deep ideological divides. Debates over reproductive rights and abortion access often result in partisan gridlock, making it challenging to reach compromise.
Immigration: Immigration policy is marked by significant partisan differences, particularly regarding issues such as border security, pathways to citizenship, and the treatment of undocumented immigrants. These divisions have hindered progress on comprehensive immigration reform.
Social Media Echo Chambers: The proliferation of social media platforms has created echo chambers where individuals are exposed primarily to information and opinions that align with their existing beliefs. This can reinforce ideological polarization and make it difficult for people to engage with differing perspectives.

Ideologically-Driven News Outlets: The rise of ideologically-driven news outlets has contributed to the polarization of media consumption. Many individuals now consume news from sources that align with their political views, further entrenching their existing beliefs and limiting exposure to diverse viewpoints.

Gerrymandering: The practice of gerrymandering, where electoral district boundaries are manipulated for partisan advantage, has created safe seats for incumbents and reduced the competitive nature of elections. This can discourage compromise and bipartisan cooperation.

Primary Elections: Primary elections often attract the most ideologically extreme voters, leading some candidates to adopt more extreme positions to secure their party's nomination. This can make it challenging for moderate candidates to gain traction and engage in bipartisan efforts. These challenges highlight the complex and deeply entrenched nature of political polarization in the United States. While bipartisanship remains a valuable goal, addressing these cracks in the bridge will require concerted efforts from both elected officials and the broader public. Finding common ground on contentious issues, promoting civil discourse, and seeking out diverse perspectives are essential steps toward bridging the divides that hinder cooperation and compromise in American politics.

Case Study: The Affordable Care Act:
The Affordable Care Act (ACA), often referred to as Obamacare, serves as a notable case study in the challenges of achieving bipartisanship on contentious issues in American politics. While the ACA aimed to expand healthcare access and address the issue of uninsured Americans, its passage through a purely Democratic process and subsequent Republican attempts to repeal it underscore the deep partisan divide surrounding healthcare reform.

Key aspects of the ACA and its relationship to bipartisanship include:

Democratic Process: The ACA was passed by Congress and signed into law by President Barack Obama in 2010 with predominantly Democratic support. The bill faced strong opposition from Republicans, who argued that it represented government overreach and raised concerns about the impact on healthcare costs and choice.

Lack of Bipartisan Support: The passage of the ACA without significant bipartisan support contributed to the perception of the law as a partisan achievement. The absence of Republican votes in favor of the bill reinforced the partisan divide on healthcare reform.

Ongoing Political Battles: Following the ACA's enactment, it became the focal point of political battles between Democrats and Republicans. Numerous attempts to repeal or undermine the law were made by Republicans, with varying degrees of success. These efforts highlighted the entrenched partisan positions on healthcare policy.

Legal Challenges: The ACA faced legal challenges, including a case that reached the Supreme Court. While the law was largely upheld, legal disputes added to the ongoing political and legal battles surrounding the ACA.

Public Opinion: Public opinion on the ACA remained deeply divided along party lines. While some Americans benefited from expanded access to healthcare coverage, others expressed concerns about the law's impact on healthcare costs and choice. This polarization extended to political leaders and policymakers.

Challenges to Bipartisanship: The ACA's contentious passage and subsequent political battles illustrated the challenges of achieving lasting bipartisanship on healthcare reform in the United States. Healthcare is a deeply personal and complex issue, and partisan divisions have made it difficult to find common ground on comprehensive healthcare solutions.

The case of the ACA serves as a cautionary tale of how deeply entrenched partisan divisions can hinder efforts to address major policy challenges, even when there is broad recognition of the need for reform. While the ACA expanded healthcare coverage for millions of Americans, it also became a symbol of the ongoing partisan divide in American politics.

Achieving bipartisanship on healthcare and other contentious issues will continue to be a significant challenge. It will require a commitment to civil discourse, finding areas of common ground, and a willingness to engage in constructive dialogue across party lines. The ACA case study serves as a reminder of the complexities of navigating these divisions and the importance of seeking bipartisan solutions to address pressing national challenges.

Obstacles on the Ladder:
Several factors threaten the stability of the bipartisan ladder. Gerrymandering, which creates safe seats for incumbents, reduces the incentive for compromise. The rise of campaign finance, where donors demand loyalty for their investments, discourages politicians from straying from party lines. Additionally, a political climate fueled by hyper-partisanship and distrust further weakens the rungs of the ladder, making collaboration seem risky and politically perilous.

The Path Forward: Mending the Broken Ladder:
Despite the challenges, the human yearning for progress compels us to seek remedies. One crucial step involves promoting transparency and fact-based discourse. Engaging diverse voices in policy discussions and fostering empathy across the divide can help rebuild trust and identify common ground. Additionally, structural reforms like independent redistricting commissions and campaign finance regulations can incentivize compromise and reduce the undue influence of special interests.

Conclusion: Beyond the Brink or Back to the Drawing Board?
The future of bipartisanship remains uncertain, and its fate
teeters on a precarious balance. Whether it evolves into a
bridge that leads to a brighter future or remains a broken
ladder that deepens division depends on our collective
determination to build connections, restore trust, and
prioritize the common good above partisan triumphs.
Although achieving bipartisanship may appear challenging,
the alternative of enduring political gridlock and societal
discord is a more daunting prospect. By nurturing the sparks
of cooperation and engaging in thoughtful, patient dialogue,
we can strive to reconstruct the ladder, rekindling faith in the
possibility of achieving collective progress across the political
spectrum.

Chapter 7: The Impact of Politics on Progress: A Dance of Progress and Peril

In the complex interplay between politics and progress, decisions dance a nuanced choreography, sometimes propelling the nation forward, other times leaving us a step closer to the brink. This chapter delves into the tangible consequences of both partisan and bipartisan choices, examining their impact on our social, economic, and environmental wellbeing, and revealing the ongoing debates that rage in their wake.

1. Social Progress: Where Lines Are Drawn and Bridges Built:

a) Partisan Crossroads: The Path to Same-Sex Marriage: The struggle for marriage equality illustrates the stark divergence of partisan perspectives on social issues. While Democrats consistently championed LGBT+ rights, Republicans largely opposed same-sex marriage, resulting in decades of legislative wrangling. Ultimately, it was a landmark Supreme Court decision in 2015, Obergefell v. Hodges, which secured nationwide marriage equality, highlighting the limitations of partisan solutions and the potential for judicial intervention to pave the way for social progress.

b) Bipartisan Collaboration: The Americans with Disabilities Act:

In contrast, the Americans with Disabilities Act (ADA) stands as a testament to the power of bipartisanship to advance social justice. Passed in 1990 under a Republican President and with strong support from both parties, the ADA outlawed discrimination against individuals with disabilities, significantly expanding their access to employment, public spaces, and opportunities. This success story reveals the potential for collaboration across party lines, especially when human rights and inclusivity are at the forefront.

2. Economic Growth: Policies of Prosperity and Polarization:

a) Tax Cuts and Trade Wars: The Republican Gamble:

The 2017 Republican tax cuts, championed by President Trump, aimed to stimulate economic growth by slashing corporate and individual taxes. However, critics argue that the benefits skewed heavily towards the wealthy, exacerbating income inequality and failing to deliver a significant boost for most Americans. Additionally, Trump's trade wars with China and other countries further clouded the economic picture, raising concerns about supply chain disruptions and economic instability. This case study exposes the complexities of economic policy, where partisan priorities can have far-reaching consequences for national prosperity and equality.

b) Infrastructure Investment: A Bipartisan Beacon in a Divided Field:
In contrast, the aforementioned Infrastructure Investment and Jobs Act serves as a beacon of hope for bipartisan economic progress. This landmark legislation, with support from both Republicans and Democrats, allocated billions for roads, bridges, and other critical infrastructure projects. While debates continue about its long-term economic impact, it undeniably represents a step towards addressing America's aging infrastructure and potentially bolstering economic activity.

3. Environmental Crossroads: Navigating the Climate Change Divide:

a) Partisan Paralysis: The Stalemate on Climate Change:
The issue of climate change exemplifies the profound chasm dividing the two parties on environmental policy. Democrats advocate for aggressive action to reduce carbon emissions and transition to renewable energy sources, while Republicans often express skepticism about the severity of the crisis and resist policy changes with significant economic implications. This partisan gridlock leaves the issue mired in political stalemates, threatening environmental progress and hindering the nation's ability to contribute meaningfully to global climate goals.

b) Bipartisan Glimmers: Clean Air and Water Legislation:
However, some hope glimmers amidst the partisan discord. The Clean Air Act and Clean Water Act, passed with bipartisan support in the 1970s, stand as enduring examples of environmental progress achieved through collaboration. These regulations, despite ongoing debates about their scope and effectiveness, have demonstrably improved air and water quality across the country, showcasing the potential for common ground on environmental issues.

Conclusion: Weighing the Costs and Dividends of Political Choices

As we navigate the intricate dance between politics and progress, it's crucial to remain cognizant of the tangible consequences of each decision. From advancing social justice to fostering economic growth and safeguarding the environment, the choices made in the political arena shape the very fabric of our nation's wellbeing. By analyzing both the successes and failures of partisan and bipartisan initiatives, we can engage in informed and constructive discussions about the path forward, striving to prioritize policies that deliver lasting progress for all Americans.

However, the debate extends beyond these well-established issues. Two topics currently ignite the American discourse, their potential consequences demanding immediate attention:

1. Abortion and Reproductive Rights: A Nation Divided

A. A Brief History of a Divided Landscape:

The landmark Roe v. Wade decision of 1973 established a woman's constitutional right to choose to terminate a pregnancy. This ruling sparked decades of ongoing legal and political battles, shaping the current landscape of reproductive rights in the United States.

Subsequent Supreme Court rulings, such as Casey v. Planned Parenthood (1992), upheld core principles of Roe but allowed states to impose certain restrictions on abortion access.

Over the past decades, states have enacted various laws regulating abortion, including waiting periods, parental consent requirements, funding restrictions for Planned Parenthood, and bans after specific gestational ages.

The Supreme Court's June 2022 decision in Dobbs v. Jackson Women's Health Organization overturned Roe v. Wade, leaving the regulation of abortion to individual states. This decision significantly altered the national landscape, igniting renewed social and political debates.

B. Demanding Choice: The Democratic Platform:

The Democratic Party platform affirms a woman's right to choose and access safe and legal abortion services. They advocate for:

Protection of Roe v. Wade principles (prior to its overturn)

Repeal of restrictive state laws and funding bans

Expansion of access to abortion services, particularly in underserved communities

Investment in comprehensive sex education and family planning programs

C. Protecting Life: The Republican Stance:
The Republican Party platform generally opposes abortion, advocating for pro-life legislation and policies aiming to reduce the number of abortions performed. They support:
Enactment of state and federal laws restricting abortion access, including bans after specific gestational ages
Defunding of Planned Parenthood and other abortion providers
Parental consent and notification requirements for minors seeking abortions.
Promotion of adoption and alternatives to abortion

D. The Human Cost of a Divided Issue:
The abortion debate has tangible consequences for women's health, economic well-being, and access to essential healthcare. Research indicates:
Women in states with restrictive abortion laws have higher maternal mortality rates than those in states with more access.
Unwanted pregnancies can lead to financial hardship, educational disruptions, and increased poverty rates.
Limited access to abortion can force women to carry unwanted pregnancies to term, with potential health risks and emotional distress.

E. Seeking Common Ground: Beyond Partisanship:
Despite the deep divide, efforts exist to seek common ground and bridge the gap between pro-choice and pro-life perspectives. These initiatives often focus on:
Factual education and information dissemination to combat misinformation and promote evidence-based understanding of abortion and its impact.
Shared values surrounding maternal health, child welfare, and reducing unwanted pregnancies.

Identifying areas of potential compromise, such as expanding access to prenatal care and social support services for pregnant women regardless of their abortion decision.

F. A Global Perspective:
Abortion access and legal frameworks vary significantly across countries. Studying international approaches can offer insights and potential learnings for the American debate.
Some countries, like Canada and most European nations, have more liberal abortion laws, allowing access upon request or with minimal restrictions.
Others, like Ireland and Poland, have stricter laws, with bans or limitations on abortion availability.
Examining diverse approaches can inform discussions about balancing individual rights, public health considerations, and cultural values.

Reimagining Abortion: Where AI and the Future Hold the Key
The abortion debate has raged for decades, seemingly entrenched in an endless clash of absolutes. But what if the answer doesn't lie in choosing sides, but in transcending the debate itself? In this crucible of ethical, emotional, and medical complexity, a glimmer of hope shines through the intersection of Artificial Intelligence and burgeoning future technologies.
Here's how AI and future tech can reimagine the problem and solution:
1. Personalized Guidance, Not Dictates: A.I. algorithms, trained on vast data sets, can analyze a woman's unique health, financial, and social circumstances to provide nuanced, non-judgmental information about the potential consequences of her choice, both for herself and her family. No longer a binary of right or wrong, abortion becomes a deeply personal journey informed by personalized data and tailored support.

2. Risk Assessment and Proactive Support: Predictive A.I. can identify women at risk for unsafe abortions or postpartum depression, proactively connecting them with necessary resources and support networks before crisis strikes. Mental health counseling, financial assistance, and even childcare alternatives, facilitated by A.I.-driven platforms, can offer a vital safety net, shifting the focus from reactive solutions to proactive prevention.

3. Destigmatizing Dialogue and Building Bridges: Imagine A.I.-powered forums where individuals on both sides of the debate can engage in respectful, fact-based conversations. By analyzing communication patterns and identifying areas of potential understanding, A.I. can help bridge the divide, fostering empathy and shared narratives through real-world data and personal stories. This shift from polarized shouting matches to nuanced dialogues can pave the way for common ground and collaborative solutions.

4. Beyond Biology: Redefining Reproduction: Emerging biotechnologies hold the potential to revolutionize the very concept of pregnancy. Imagine implants or ingestibles that offer complete control over fertility cycles, allowing women to pause or rewind their biological clocks. This wouldn't just eliminate unwanted pregnancies, it would empower women to design their own reproductive timelines, shattering traditional notions of motherhood and societal expectations.

5. The Empathy Network: Rekindling Human Connection: In a world of algorithms and screens, we forget the human core of the abortion debate. A.I. can facilitate connections between women facing difficult choices and potential adoptive families, creating a virtual space for shared stories, fears, and hopes. This radical act of empathy, driven by AI but fueled by human connection, could transform the landscape of abortion, leading to mutually beneficial outcomes for all involved.

Of course, these ideas are just the tip of the iceberg. Ethical considerations, technical hurdles, and societal anxieties will need to be navigated. But by stepping outside the box and embracing the potential of AI and future tech, we can move beyond the rigidity of the current debate and reimagine a future where women's autonomy, informed by technology and fueled by empathy, takes center stage.

This is not about finding a "solution" in the traditional sense. It's about opening a door to a future where the very way we think about abortion, reproduction, and choice is transformed. AI and future tech offer not a definitive answer, but a toolkit for reimagining the problem itself, shifting the conversation from pro-choice versus pro-life to a more nuanced, human-centered approach.

Let's continue exploring these possibilities, pushing the boundaries of what we think is possible, and crafting a future where women's well-being and personal agency are at the heart of the reproductive conversation. The human journey is full of unexpected twists and turns, and when it comes to this sensitive issue, perhaps the most profound solutions lie not in rigid positions, but in the power of imagination and the endless possibilities offered by a future yet to be written.

2. *Navigating the Gunfire: America's Enduring Struggle with Gun Control*

From colonial muskets to high-powered AR-15s, the gun has carved a deep and controversial path through American history. The right to bear arms, enshrined in the Second Amendment, is fiercely defended by some, while others cry out for stricter regulations in the face of a nation plagued by gun violence. This chapter delves into the historical roots, global comparisons, and ongoing debate surrounding gun control in America, offering a nuanced perspective on a complex issue that shapes the nation's very fabric.

From Self-Reliance to Regulation:
Gun ownership in America has mirrored its evolving identity. Colonists viewed guns as tools for survival and defense against perceived threats, leading to minimal regulations. The Wild West era solidified the romanticized image of unfettered gun ownership, though local laws addressed firearm use in specific contexts. However, the 20th century saw a shift towards regulation. The National Firearms Act (1934) aimed to curb organized crime, while the Gun Control Act (1968) established federal firearm licensing and the Brady Handgun Violence Prevention Act (1993) mandated background checks for handgun purchases.

A Global Lens: Lessons Learned and Comparisons Made:
Looking beyond American borders reveals nations experiencing significantly lower gun violence rates thanks to stricter regulations. Australia's 1996 buyback program following a mass shooting demonstrably decreased gun violence, while Switzerland, despite widespread gun ownership, maintains low rates due to mandatory military service and stringent ownership rules. These comparisons offer valuable insights, while also acknowledging the unique cultural and historical context of the United States.

The Divided Debate: Arguments and Impacts:
Proponents of gun control, often aligned with the Democratic party, prioritize public safety and argue for:
Background checks: Expanding them to private sales and transfers could prevent gun deaths, particularly suicides and domestic violence homicides.
Assault weapons bans: Limiting access to these high-powered firearms could decrease the lethality of mass shootings.
Mental health initiatives: Addressing mental health concerns alongside gun control is seen as a comprehensive approach to violence prevention.
However, strong opposition, often from Republicans, emphasizes individual liberty and argues against stricter regulations due to:
Constitutional concerns: Many believe stricter gun control infringes on the Second Amendment right to bear arms and fear government overreach.
Ineffectiveness of laws: Opponents argue that existing laws fail to address the root causes of gun violence, like mental health concerns or socioeconomic issues, and disproportionately burden law-abiding citizens.
Responsible gun ownership: They advocate for education and training programs to promote responsible gun ownership instead of stricter regulations.

Both sides point to evidence supporting their arguments, creating a climate of gridlock and frustration. While gun control advocates cite studies showing the effectiveness of background checks in preventing gun deaths, opponents highlight examples where existing laws failed to stop criminals. This lack of consensus and the entrenched nature of both sides' positions present a significant challenge to progress.

Finding Common Ground Amidst the Strife:
Despite the apparent divide, potential paths forward exist. Areas of bipartisan compromise could include:
Universal background checks: Expanding background checks to cover private sales and transfers could find agreement from moderate members of both parties.
Investment in mental health: Addressing mental health concerns alongside gun control measures could gain broader support, acknowledging the complex factors contributing to gun violence.
Gun safety education: Promoting responsible gun ownership through education and training programs could benefit both gun owners and non-gun owners alike.
However, the influence of political parties often hinders progress. Partisan divides tend to solidify along ideological lines, with Democrats largely supporting stricter gun control and Republicans largely opposing it. This political polarization makes finding common ground and crafting effective legislation a constant uphill battle.

Moving Forward: A Nation at a Crossroads:

The gun control debate remains a complex and emotionally charged issue with no easy answers. It calls for a nuanced understanding of diverse perspectives, an informed analysis of data and evidence, and a willingness to prioritize solutions that enhance public safety without infringing on fundamental rights. This chapter has offered a glimpse into the historical roots, global comparisons, and ongoing struggle surrounding gun control in America. It is but a springboard for further exploration, a call to engage in civil discourse and seek common ground amidst the gunfire. Only then can we hope to chart a path towards a future where the echoes of violence are replaced by the shared voices of a nation striving for a safer tomorrow.

Beyond Bullets and Borders: Reimagining Gun Control with AI and Future Tech

As we stand at the crossroads of the gun control debate, amidst gridlock and the heartbreak of gun violence, a glimmer of hope emerges: the potential of AI and future tech to reshape the problem and its solutions. Here, we explore how these transformative forces can redefine how we think about guns, safety, and responsible ownership.

1. The All-Seeing Eye: Proactive Risk Assessment and Prevention

Imagine AI algorithms analyzing social media behavior, criminal records, and mental health indicators to identify individuals at risk of committing gun violence. This proactive approach could involve:

Early intervention: Flagging high-risk individuals for mental health support or community outreach before resorting to reactive measures.

Smart gun technology: Firearms incorporating biometric locks or disabling mechanisms activated when in the wrong hands, preventing unauthorized use.

Predictive policing: AI-powered systems analyzing crime patterns and gun-related activity to anticipate and prevent potential shootings.

These technologies raise ethical concerns about privacy and potential misuse, necessitating stringent safeguards and open dialogue. However, the potential to prevent tragedies before they occur, saving lives and fostering safer communities, is undeniable.

2. Beyond Background Checks: Real-Time Verification and Transparency

Current background checks rely on existing databases, often incomplete or outdated. AI can revolutionize this system by:

Real-time verification: Instantly checking an individual's eligibility to purchase a firearm against comprehensive, continuously updated databases, including mental health records and red flags.

Blockchain-based gun registries: Secure, transparent record-keeping of firearm ownership using blockchain technology, facilitating tracing and accountability.

AI-powered gun identification: Smart cameras linked to AI systems automatically identifying and reporting illegal gun use in public spaces.

These innovations can streamline the verification process, deter illegal gun ownership, and improve overall transparency, contributing to a safer gun environment.

3. Destigmatizing the Dialogue: AI-Facilitated Discussions and Empathy Building

The gun control debate is often polarized and emotionally charged. AI can help bridge the divide by:

AI-powered forums: Providing safe spaces for respectful dialogue between gun owners, gun violence victims, and policymakers, facilitated by AI algorithms that guide discussions and highlight common ground.

Empathy AI: Personalized simulations allowing individuals to experience the impact of gun violence from different perspectives, fostering understanding and potentially shifting entrenched viewpoints.

Fact-checking and misinformation control: AI tools identifying and flagging misinformation around gun control, promoting informed decision-making and preventing the spread of harmful narratives.

By fostering open, evidence-based dialogue and building empathy, AI can move us beyond the shouting matches and towards collaborative solutions.

4. Redefining the Gun Itself: Exploring Non-Lethal Alternatives

Future tech holds the potential to revolutionize firearms themselves. Imagine:

Non-lethal personal defense weapons: High-tech alternatives to traditional firearms, like directed energy weapons or advanced tasers, offering effective self-defense without potentially lethal consequences.

Smart ammunition: Bullets programmed to disable themselves after a certain distance or upon unauthorized use, minimizing potential harm and collateral damage.

Biometric ammunition: Ammunition only functional when fired by the authorized owner, deterring theft and unauthorized use.

These futuristic concepts raise numerous ethical and technical challenges, but they offer a glimpse into a world where the very definition of a "gun" is transformed, potentially shifting the landscape of gun violence prevention.

The Responsibility Remains Human:

While AI and future tech offer transformative possibilities, remembering that the solutions ultimately lie with us is crucial. We must be vigilant in ensuring these technologies are developed and implemented ethically, prioritizing transparency, accountability, and human oversight. It is our responsibility to harness the potential of AI for good, shaping a future where gun violence is not an accepted reality, but a distant memory.

5. Moving Forward: Finding Common Ground in a Divided Landscape:

In today's increasingly polarized political environment, finding common ground and fostering constructive dialogue is more crucial than ever. This requires a concerted effort to recognize and build upon shared values and seek areas where compromise is possible. Engaging in respectful, fact-based discourse is essential to navigate the complexities of American politics effectively. By focusing on common goals and interests, such as the overall well-being of the citizenry and the nation's prosperity, and by being open to understanding and considering differing viewpoints, there is potential to bridge divides. This approach is vital not only for effective governance but also for maintaining a healthy democratic society where diverse opinions are heard and valued.

Chapter 8: Echoes in the River of Time: Navigating the River of Power in American Politics

The American political landscape, much like a mighty river, whispers with echoes of past empires and vanished ideologies. This chapter embarks on a historical voyage, not solely upstream within our national borders, but across continents and millennia. We draw comparisons between the Democratic, Republican, and third-party movements with their predecessors from diverse periods and regions, illuminating their turns as the dominant force. By examining their triumphs and pitfalls, progress and downfall, we seek lessons for the future of American politics, navigating the tumultuous river of power.

1. Democrats: Embracing Change, Weathering Storms:

Ancient Athenian Democracy (5th century BC): A beacon of direct citizen participation, the Athenian model resonates with the Democrats' emphasis on social justice and inclusion. Pros: Innovation in art and philosophy, direct engagement from the populace. Cons: Vulnerability to external threats, susceptibility to demagoguery. Lessons: Balancing individual rights with national security, prioritizing informed citizenry. Medieval Islamic Caliphates (7th-13th centuries AD): Blending religious doctrine with governance, the Caliphate echoes the Democrats' historical alliance with faith-based communities. Pros: Advancement in science and mathematics, religious tolerance across diverse faiths. Cons: Internal power struggles, intolerance towards dissenters. Lessons: Navigating the relationship between religion and state, upholding religious freedom while seeking common ground.

Modern Social Democratic Parties (20th-21st centuries): European models like Sweden and Germany offer contemporary parallels to the Democrats' focus on social safety nets and economic equality. Pros: Reduced poverty, high levels of education and healthcare. Cons: Potential for fiscal imbalance, bureaucratic inefficiencies. Lessons: Balancing social welfare with economic sustainability, seeking workable solutions for income inequality.

2. Republicans: From Unity to Division:

Roman Republic (509-31 BC): A blend of aristocratic rule and elected officials, the Roman Republic resonates with the Republicans' emphasis on limited government and individual freedoms. Pros: Stability and prosperity during its zenith, innovations in law and infrastructure. Cons: Growing inequality, political corruption, eventual descent into civil war. Lessons: Maintaining checks and balances within the system, safeguarding against the concentration of power, upholding ethical standards in governance.
Confucian China (500 BCE-1912 CE): With an emphasis on order, hierarchy, and meritocracy, ancient China offers parallels to the Republicans' focus on fiscal responsibility and social conservatism. Pros: Long periods of stability and cultural flourishing, emphasis on education and hard work. Cons: Rigid social structures limited political participation, susceptibility to corruption. Lessons: Balancing order with individual liberties, promoting upward mobility while addressing systemic inequalities.

Modern Conservative Parties (20th-21st centuries): Margaret Thatcher's Britain and the Reagan era in the US offer contemporary parallels to the Republicans' focus on deregulation and free markets. Pros: Economic growth, reduced government intervention. Cons: Widening income gap, social and environmental concerns. Lessons: Finding the right balance between economic freedom and social responsibility, addressing the impacts of globalization and technological advancements.

3. Third-Party Tides: Flashes of Brilliance, Struggles for Endurance:

Populist Movements (19th-21st centuries): From the American Populists to Gandhi's Swaraj movement in India, these movements share the third-party spirit of challenging entrenched elites and advocating for the marginalized. Pros: Bringing new voices and perspectives to the table, tackling issues ignored by existing parties. Cons: Difficulty in forming cohesive platforms, susceptibility to fragmentation and short-lived success. Lessons: The power of grassroots movements, fostering inclusivity and addressing the concerns of disenfranchised groups.
Utopian Experiments (throughout history): From Plato's Republic to Thomas More's Utopia, these visions of ideal societies offer parallels to the third-party aspirations for reshaping political systems. Pros: Bold ideas for social reforms, questioning existing paradigms. Cons: Difficulty in practical implementation, potential for unintended consequences. Lessons: The importance of critical thinking and long-term planning, balancing idealism with pragmatic considerations.

Modern Green Parties (20th-21st centuries): Focusing on environmentalism and sustainability, these parties offer a growing challenge to the traditional two-party duopoly. Pros: Raising awareness of critical issues, pushing for environmental reforms. Cons: Difficulty in balancing environmental concerns with economic realities, attracting broader support beyond a niche base. Lessons: The value of addressing pressing global challenges, finding common ground on environmental issues despite ideological differences.

Conclusion: Echoes in the River of Time

As we navigate the rapids of the American political river, studying the triumphs and pitfalls of dominant parties across history offers a treasure map for the future. We learn that internal divisions, while challenging, can lead to stronger platforms and broader appeal, as the Democrats' evolution from Jeffersonian agrarians to champions of social justice demonstrates. We witness the transformative power of external pressure, as the Civil Rights Movement reshaped the Democratic Party's stance on racial equality.

Similarly, the Republican Party's journey reveals the cyclical nature of internal strife. From Lincoln's unifying leadership to the Tea Party's challenge to the "establishment," we see the delicate balance between ideological purity and pragmatic compromise. Reagan's rise illustrates the ability of charismatic leaders to reshape party priorities and mobilize new generations.

Third-party movements, though often short-lived, offer flashes of brilliance. The Populists raised crucial questions about economic inequality, while the Progressive Republicans championed conservation and trust-busting. The Green Party's struggle to balance environmental concerns with economic realities mirrors the challenges faced by all third-party movements seeking to break the two-party stranglehold.

The echoes of history resonate further as we compare American parties to their counterparts across time and space. The Athenian Democracy's direct citizen participation echoes the Democrats' emphasis on inclusion, while the Roman Republic's blend of aristocratic rule and elected officials mirrors the Republicans' focus on limited government. The medieval Islamic Caliphates' religious influence resonates with the Democrats' historical alliance with faith-based communities, while ancient China's emphasis on order and meritocracy offers parallels to the Republicans' social conservatism.

Studying these echoes of power across time and place equips us with a critical lens to analyze the American political landscape. We recognize the cyclical nature of ideological shifts, the influence of external pressures, and the potential for both progress and downfall within every dominant party.

This understanding empowers us to engage more thoughtfully with contemporary political discourse, fostering informed civic participation and striving for a future where political parties serve not just power and ideology, but the collective good of the American people.

The river of American politics will continue to flow, carrying with it the echoes of past triumphs and failures. By embracing the lessons of history, we can navigate its rapids with wisdom and purpose, shaping a future where every citizen, regardless of party affiliation, feels empowered to contribute to a more just and equitable society.

Chapter 9: The Evolving Political Theater: Communication, Polarization, and Engagement in the Age of Technology

The American political landscape has always been a vibrant stage, but the rise of technology, media, and social media has transformed it into a dynamic and sometimes chaotic theater. This chapter delves into the backstage and onto the center stage, examining how these powerful forces have altered the ways we communicate, interact, and engage with the political sphere.

1. From Parchment to Pixels: The Revolution in Communication:

Gone are the days of town criers and handwritten letters. Today, political messages travel at the speed of light, carried on invisible waves by smartphones, computers, and the ever-expanding digital universe. This revolution in communication has brought undeniable benefits. Politicians can now reach vast audiences instantly, bypassing traditional gatekeepers and fostering a sense of direct connection with the electorate. Social media platforms have democratized the flow of information, allowing individuals to amplify their voices and challenge the narratives spun by entrenched powers. However, this accessibility comes at a cost. The sheer volume of information can be overwhelming, leading to confusion and the spread of misinformation. "Filter bubbles" and echo chambers created by algorithms reinforce existing biases and hinder healthy cross-ideological discourse. The 24/7 news cycle thrives on sensationalism and negativity, fueling political polarization and eroding trust in institutions.

2. From Town Squares to Tweets: The Polarization Paradox:

While technology promised to connect us, it has arguably exacerbated partisan divides. Social media algorithms designed to maximize engagement often prioritize content that provokes anger or outrage, creating echo chambers where users encounter only those who validate their existing beliefs. Political discourse devolves into tribal warfare, with vitriol and misinformation masquerading as informed debate. This polarization not only hampers constructive policymaking but also erodes our sense of shared national identity, creating a fractured political landscape where dialogue feels like a lost art.

3. From Spectators to Participants: The Public Engagement Puzzle:

Technology has undeniably increased the avenues for public engagement in politics. Social media allows individuals to directly express their opinions, advocate for causes, and mobilize communities. Online petitions and crowd-funding campaigns empower citizens to influence policy agendas and bypass traditional power structures. This participatory potential holds immense promise for a more responsive and accountable democracy.
Yet, challenges remain. Digital divides limit access for disadvantaged communities, perpetuating existing inequalities. Cyberbullying and online harassment deter meaningful participation, especially for women and minorities. The sheer volume of voices can be overwhelming, making it difficult to discern genuine grassroots movements from astroturf campaigns and manipulative bots.

Navigating the Evolving Stage:

The political theater continues to evolve, shaped by the ever-changing tides of technology, media, and social media. To navigate this complex landscape, we need a multifaceted approach. Politicians must embrace transparency and authenticity, engaging in genuine dialogue with citizens rather than resorting to manipulative tactics. Media outlets must prioritize factual reporting and foster nuanced discussions, resisting the siren song of sensationalism. Social media platforms must prioritize algorithms that foster healthy exchange and combat misinformation.

Most importantly, the onus lies on us, the citizens. We must equip ourselves with critical thinking skills to discern fact from fiction, engage in respectful dialogue across ideological divides, and hold both ourselves and our leaders accountable. Only by becoming active participants in this evolving political theater can we ensure that it serves the needs of all, not just the loudest or most powerful voices.

The curtain is rising on a new act in the American political landscape. Will it be a drama of division and discord, or a collaborative performance guided by informed engagement and civic virtue? The answer lies in our hands, as we each step onto the stage and take our turn in this ever-evolving political theater.

Part 3: Future Visions and Possibilities

Chapter 10: Demo-lib-public or Transformation? Unmasking the American Political Trifecta

The American political landscape stands poised on a precarious precipice, with the three major players - Democrats, Republicans, and third-party movements - each grappling with existential questions and potential fractures. This chapter delves into the intricate underbelly of these parties, unveiling their internal and external battlegrounds, and posing the crucial question: are they heading for a political demolition derby or a transformative rebirth?

1. Democrats: Juggling Progress and Party Unity:
Internal Clash of Ideals: Bernie Sanders' progressive resurgence exposes a widening chasm between moderates and liberals within the party. The Green New Deal's bold climate proposals find lukewarm support among centrists, while healthcare reform debates pit Medicare-for-All advocates against incrementalists. These fissures erupted during the 2020 primary, highlighting the precarious balancing act required to keep the coalition together.
External Pressures from Social and Economic Fronts: Rising inflation, fueled by global supply chain disruptions and the Ukraine war, has eroded public confidence in Democratic economic stewardship. Social movements, while crucial allies, can also alienate swing voters. The Black Lives Matter protests, while sparking necessary conversations about racial justice, provoked backlash from conservative segments, pushing moderate Democrats onto the defensive.

Navigating the Crossroads: To avoid disintegration, Democrats must bridge internal divides by crafting policies that address economic anxieties while staying true to progressive values. Finding consensus on climate change action, without alienating rural communities, or striking a balance on healthcare that expands access while respecting moderate concerns, will be critical. Success hinges on articulating a compelling vision for the future that unites their diverse base and attracts new voters.

2. Republicans: Torn Between Trumpism and Traditionalism:

The Post-Trump Fissures: The former president's grip on the party remains, evidenced by his endorsement power and the loyalty of MAGA Republicans. This clashes with traditional conservatives who yearn for a return to pre-Trump ideals. Issues like immigration and election integrity expose these divisions, with hardliners demanding stricter measures while moderates seek compromise. The future leadership of the party hangs in the balance, hinging on whether Trumpism remains dominant or traditional Republicans regain control. Demographic Shifts and Economic Unease: The party's traditional base faces challenges from demographic shifts, particularly the growing Latino and Asian populations. Climate change concerns resonate with younger voters, but the party's response often appears out of touch. Economic woes, especially in rural areas, leave Republicans vulnerable to populist appeals, further complicating their efforts to attract a broader electorate.

Adaptation or irrelevance: To ensure long-term viability, Republicans must reconcile their factions. Embracing inclusivity and adapting to demographic changes are crucial, as is crafting policy stances that address climate concerns without alienating their base. Failure to do so could lead to further fracturing and irrelevance in a changing America.

3. Third-Party Tides: Riding the Waves of Dissatisfaction:
The Struggle for Unity and Visibility: From the Green Party's environmental focus to the Libertarians' championing of individual liberty, third-party movements offer diverse perspectives. However, unifying these platforms proves difficult, with Bernie Sanders' independent run in 2016 highlighting the challenges of bridging ideological gaps. Lack of funding and media access further hinders their ability to reach a wider audience.
Strategic Alliances and Grassroots Movements: The Green Party's collaboration with other progressive groups on environmental issues like the Clean Power Plan demonstrates the potential of strategic alliances. Bernie Sanders' success in mobilizing grassroots support offers another lesson for third-party movements seeking to break through the duopoly's stranglehold.
Breaking the Duopoly or Breaking Apart? To gain traction, third-party movements need to coalesce around core issues, present a united front, and build strong grassroots movements. Leveraging social media effectively and forging strategic alliances with other progressive or conservative groups can amplify their voices. However, continued disunity and inability to overcome the two-party barrier could lead to further decline and irrelevance.

4. Looming Shadows on the Political Landscape:

Beyond internal struggles, external factors cast long shadows across the political landscape:

Technological Disruption: Social media's influence on political discourse, the rise of misinformation, and the potential for foreign interference pose challenges for all parties. Finding ways to combat online toxicity and misinformation while harnessing the potential of technology for civic engagement will be crucial.

Global Challenges: Climate change, economic inequality, and geopolitical instability demand collaborative solutions. Can the parties transcend partisan divides to address these issues, or will they become further entrenched in their respective camps?

The Shifting Electorate: Demographic changes, evolving social values, and growing youth activism demand attention and responsive platforms. How will the parties adapt to meet the needs of a changing electorate and remain relevant in the years to come?

Conclusion: A Crossroads of Choices, a Crucible of Transformation

The American political trilemma stands at a pivotal juncture, teetering between demolition and transformation. The Democrats grapple with balancing progressive ideals against economic anxieties, the Republicans confront a fractured identity between Trumpism and tradition, and third-party movements struggle to break the ironclad grip of the two-party system. The choices they make in the face of internal fissures and external pressures will not only determine their own fates but also shape the very future of American democracy.

Scenarios of Transformation:

The Pragmatic Democrats: If Democrats can successfully bridge internal divides, craft policies that address economic anxieties while championing progressive values, and articulate a compelling vision for the future, they could consolidate their base and attract new voters, emerging stronger and more unified.

The Evolving Republicans: If Republicans can reconcile their factions, embrace inclusivity, adapt to demographic shifts, and present solutions that address climate concerns without alienating their base, they could regain relevance in a changing America and reclaim their role as a centrist alternative.

The Green Surge: If third-party movements can overcome their internal divisions, coalesce around core issues, leverage technology effectively, and build strong grassroots movements, they could potentially break the duopoly's hold and inject fresh perspectives into the political discourse.

Scenarios of Demo-Lib-Public:

The Fractured Democrats: If internal ideological clashes escalate, moderate Democrats alienate the progressive base, and economic anxieties remain unaddressed, the party could face further fragmentation, diminishing their political effectiveness.

The Trumpified Republicans: If Republicans succumb to the allure of Trumpism, fail to adapt to demographic shifts, and remain entrenched in outdated stances on issues like climate change, they risk further alienating swing voters and becoming increasingly irrelevant in a diversifying nation.

The Fading Third Parties: If internal disunity persists, funding and media access remain limited, and strategic alliances fail to materialize, third-party movements could fade into further obscurity, leaving the two-party system undisturbed.

The journey ahead will be fraught with challenges, but it also holds immense potential for transformation. Whether America witnesses a revitalized political landscape where diverse voices are heard and common ground is sought, or a descent into further polarization and dysfunction, depends on the choices made by the players in this grand political drama. The curtain has risen on Act III, and it is up to the American people to become active participants, ensuring that the story unfolds towards a brighter and more inclusive future.

Chapter 11: Survival, Expansion, or Merging? Charting the Future of the American Political Trifecta

As the American political landscape undergoes constant seismic shifts, the fates of the three major players - Democrats, Republicans, and third-party movements - hang in the balance. This chapter delves into the realm of possibilities, offering well-researched and logically supported predictions about their potential futures, encompassing scenarios for survival, expansion, decline, and even the unthinkable: merging. Buckle up, for we embark on a journey into the uncharted territory of American politics, where the lines between survival and extinction are constantly being redrawn.

1. Democrats: Navigating the Tightrope of Unity and Progress:

Survival Scenario: The Democrats' future hinges on their ability to bridge the widening chasm between progressive and moderate wings. Finding common ground on critical issues like climate change, healthcare, and economic policy, while prioritizing pragmatism without sacrificing core values, could lead to a unified party attracting broader support. Embracing technological advancements for grassroots organizing and effective messaging can further solidify their base and attract new voters. Additionally, capitalizing on growing demographic shifts, particularly among younger generations and minority communities, could secure long-term viability.

Expansion Scenario: A bold vision for the future, coupled with charismatic leadership that rallies the base and resonates with swing voters, could propel the Democrats towards expansion. Championing social justice movements and addressing economic anxieties with innovative solutions could broaden their appeal. Strategic alliances with progressive third-party groups and labor unions could further expand their reach and leverage collective bargaining power. Success in addressing global challenges like climate change and economic inequality could solidify their position as a global leader, fostering international partnerships and alliances.

Decline Scenario: Failure to bridge internal divisions could lead to further fractures, as progressive and moderate wings splinter into separate entities. Economic woes, exacerbated by external factors like global instability, could erode public trust and fuel discontent within the base. Ineffectiveness in addressing social justice concerns could alienate minority communities, while a perceived disconnect from rural concerns could further shrink their electoral map. Technological advancements, if exploited by misinformation campaigns and foreign interference, could undermine public trust and democratic processes, further jeopardizing their hold on power.

Merging Scenario: While seemingly improbable, a political realignment triggered by unforeseen events like catastrophic economic turmoil or social unrest could lead to a merging of the Democratic and progressive wings of the political spectrum. Such a merger would result in a formidable center-left force, potentially reshaping the two-party system and challenging traditional notions of American political ideology.

2. *Republicans: Between Trumpism and Tradition:*

Survival Scenario: The Republican Party's survival hinges on reconciling its factions. Embracing inclusivity and adapting to demographic shifts are crucial. Moderates need to reclaim control from the grip of Trumpism, offering alternative visions that address climate concerns, economic anxieties, and social justice issues without alienating their base. Leveraging technological advancements for targeted outreach and effective messaging can help them regain relevancy among younger voters and minority communities. A renewed focus on fiscal responsibility and national security, while addressing concerns about corruption and income inequality, could solidify their appeal among traditional conservative voters.

Expansion Scenario: A charismatic leader who bridges the gap between moderates and Trump supporters, offering a unifying vision for the future while upholding conservative values, could propel the Republicans towards expansion. Embracing technological advancements for fundraising and campaigning can enhance their reach and effectiveness. Strategically aligning with religious groups and rural communities on issues like abortion and gun rights could solidify their traditional base. Success in tackling economic challenges and foreign policy issues could bolster their image as a strong and competent governing force, attracting swing voters.

Decline Scenario: Continued infighting between Trump loyalists and traditional Republicans could lead to further fractures, weakening their collective power. Ignoring demographic shifts and clinging to outdated stances on social issues could alienate younger voters and minority communities. Failure to address economic anxieties and the growing gap between rich and poor could erode their support among working-class voters. Technological advancements, if exploited by misinformation campaigns and foreign interference, could exacerbate internal divisions and further erode public trust.

Merging Scenario: Similar to the Democrats, a realignment triggered by unforeseen events could lead to a merger between traditional Republicans and disaffected Trump supporters. This hypothetical scenario would result in a center-right force, potentially reshaping the two-party system and offering a conservative alternative that addresses contemporary concerns.

3. Third-Party Tides: Breaking the Duopoly or Breaking Apart?

Survival Scenario: To break the duopoly's stranglehold, third-party movements need to overcome internal divisions and coalesce around core issues like climate change, economic inequality, and social justice. Strategic alliances with other like-minded groups, both progressive and conservative, can amplify their voices and increase their visibility. Leveraging social media effectively for grassroots organizing and targeted outreach can bypass traditional media gatekeepers and reach new audiences. Success in local and state elections, even small victories, can build momentum and attract resources and funding: Traditional third-party struggles often stem from limited financial resources. Exploring innovative fundraising models like crowdfunding and small-donor contributions can fuel their campaigns. Cultivating relationships with like-minded philanthropists and businesses can provide additional support.
*Embrace the power of "the issue": By focusing on specific, well-defined issues like environmental protection, campaign finance reform, or electoral systems reform, third parties can appeal to a passionate base without needing a comprehensive platform. This laser-sharp focus can attract disaffected voters from both major parties.
*Cultivate charismatic leaders: Third-party movements often lack the national figures that major parties leverage. Identifying and nurturing charismatic leaders who embody their values and resonate with voters can be a game-changer. These leaders can become the public face of the movement, attracting media attention and mobilizing supporters.

Expansion Scenario: Riding a wave of dissatisfaction: Significant public disillusionment with both major parties could create fertile ground for third-party expansion. Capitalizing on voter anger towards gridlock, corruption, or failed policies can attract a disenfranchised electorate seeking alternatives.

The power of protest movements: Social movements advocating for racial justice, environmental protection, or economic equality can provide a springboard for third-party growth. By strategically aligning with and amplifying these movements' voices, third parties can tap into existing networks and reach passionate supporters.

Evolving demographics and shifting ideologies: Demographic shifts and changing social values, particularly among younger generations, can create openings for third-party expansion. Embracing progressive stances on issues like LGBTQ+ rights, climate change, and gun control can resonate with this growing segment of the electorate.

Decline Scenario: Fractured ideals and competing visions: Internal divisions within third-party movements can be their undoing. Inability to find common ground on core issues, or ideological clashes between factions, can lead to splintering and weaken their collective impact.

The two-party stranglehold: The entrenched system of electoral funding, media access, and voter habits can be formidable barriers for third-party candidates. Lacking the resources and infrastructure of major parties, they may struggle to reach voters and compete effectively.

The spoiler effect: Even if they don't win elections, third-party candidates can play the spoiler role, drawing votes away from the major parties and potentially tipping the balance in close races. This can alienate voters who prioritize defeating their preferred party's opponent over ideological purity.

Merging Scenario: While less likely compared to the two major parties, third-party movements could potentially merge, forming a larger force on the political spectrum. This could happen if diverse third-party groups find common ground on core issues and recognize the strategic benefits of consolidation. A hypothetical merger could create a strong center-left or center-right force, challenging the existing duopoly and offering voters a distinct alternative.

Beyond the Binary

Ultimately, the future of the American political landscape remains a kaleidoscope of possibilities. While the scenarios presented in this chapter offer plausible trajectories, unforeseen events and evolving social dynamics can alter the course dramatically. The survival, expansion, or potential merging of these parties hinge not just on internal dynamics but also on the choices of the American electorate. Whether voters embrace pragmatism, seek ideological purity, or yearn for a complete overhaul of the system, their voices will ultimately determine the shape of the political landscape to come.

Chapter 12: The Rise of AI in Governance: Friend or Foe on the Political Stage?

The digital revolution is not just transforming economies and social interaction; it's also knocking on the doors of the political sphere, raising provocative questions about the future of governance. Artificial intelligence (AI), once the stuff of science fiction, now stands poised to play a transformative role in the way we elect, legislate, and even run our societies. This chapter delves into the intricate dance between AI and governance, exploring its potential benefits and drawbacks, ethical dilemmas, and the impact it could have on the very fabric of traditional party structures.

AI: The Digital Hand in the Ballot Box:

The Algorithm as Kingmaker: Imagine campaign strategies meticulously calibrated by real-time sentiment analysis, micro-targeted voter outreach optimized with laser precision, and election predictions based on vast and intricate datasets. AI promises to revolutionize campaign dynamics, potentially making them more efficient and responsive to voter needs. Personalized ads tailored to individual voters' concerns could replace blanket messaging, increasing engagement and potentially boosting voter turnout. However, this algorithmic precision comes with a dark side: concerns about bias and manipulation loom large. Unchecked, AI-powered campaigns could exacerbate existing societal inequalities, disenfranchise minority groups, and even spread misinformation to sway voters. The very promise of efficiency could create echo chambers, further polarizing the political landscape.

The Citizen's Digital Town Hall: AI-powered platforms could usher in an era of direct democracy, facilitating real-time feedback from citizens on policy decisions and fostering ongoing dialogue between constituents and their elected officials. Imagine town halls happening online, with AI analyzing public sentiment and translating it into actionable insights for lawmakers. Imagine policy proposals crowdsourced and refined through iterative feedback loops with the electorate. Such platforms could foster a more inclusive and responsive form of governance, empowering citizens to actively participate in shaping their communities. However, ensuring equitable access to these platforms becomes crucial. Rural communities or marginalized groups lacking digital literacy could be easily excluded from this digital civic square, widening the existing digital divide and further disenfranchising vulnerable populations.

The Efficiency Engine: From streamlining administrative tasks to analyzing complex policy outcomes, AI has the potential to significantly improve the efficiency and effectiveness of government. Automating routine processes like tax filing or permit applications could free up resources for lawmakers to focus on more strategic issues, while predictive analytics could inform evidence-based policy decisions. Imagine AI analyzing economic data to predict unemployment trends and proactively create safety nets, or using sentiment analysis to identify areas of public dissatisfaction and address them before they escalate into protests. However, concerns regarding algorithmic opacity and human accountability in critical decision-making processes must be addressed. Who is liable when an AI-driven policy backfires? Who oversees the algorithms making decisions that impact millions of lives? These questions demand clear answers before we fully embrace the efficiency engine of AI in governance.

A Double-Edged Sword: The Drawbacks and Dangers of AI in Governance:

The Erosion of Human Trust: With algorithms making decisions behind the scenes, citizens may feel increasingly distanced from their elected officials and question the transparency of decision-making processes. This lack of trust could erode public confidence in government and lead to apathy or dissent. Imagine a scenario where an AI-powered algorithm denies someone social benefits based on opaque criteria, leaving the individual with no recourse or understanding of the decision. Such scenarios could fuel feelings of alienation and distrust, ultimately weakening the very bedrock of democracy.

The Bias Algorithm: AI algorithms, like any tool, are only as good as the data they are trained on. Biases within datasets can be amplified by AI, leading to discriminatory outcomes in areas like criminal justice, resource allocation, and policy implementation. Imagine an AI-powered risk assessment tool used for parole decisions systematically biased against minority groups, leading to unfair incarceration rates. Such scenarios highlight the urgency of addressing algorithmic bias head-on. We must ensure datasets are representative and diverse and develop mechanisms to detect and mitigate bias throughout the AI development and deployment processes.

The Algorithmic Overlords: The potential for AI to become too powerful, making decisions autonomously without human oversight, raises dystopian concerns. The line between AI as a powerful tool and AI as a potential puppeteer needs to be clearly defined and constantly monitored. Imagine an AI system controlling critical infrastructure like traffic lights or power grids, vulnerable to hacking or malfunctioning with potentially catastrophic consequences. Such scenarios are not the stuff of science fiction; they are serious considerations that demand robust safeguards and emergency protocols.

Navigating the Ethical Minefield:
Developing and deploying AI in governance demands a robust ethical framework, not just a set of principles, but a living document constantly evolving with the technology. Principles like transparency, accountability, fairness, and human oversight must be more than buzzwords, imbued into every stage of the process. Public education and open dialogue about the potential and limitations of AI in government are crucial for building trust and ensuring responsible implementation. This cannot be a one-sided conversation held within government chambers; it must involve citizens in co-designing ethical frameworks and understanding the algorithms impacting their lives.

Let's delve deeper into these crucial components:

1. **Data** Privacy: Transparent data collection and usage guidelines are paramount. Citizens must understand how their data is being used, by whom, and for what purpose. Opt-in and opt-out mechanisms must be readily available, giving individuals control over their digital footprints. Data anonymization techniques and strong cybersecurity measures are essential to prevent misuse and ensure privacy.

2. **Algorithmic Auditing**: Algorithms are not magic boxes; they are complex models built on datasets, and like any tool, they can be biased. Robust algorithmic auditing mechanisms are needed to detect and mitigate bias in data, algorithms themselves, and their outputs. Independent auditors, not those involved in developing the algorithms, should regularly scrutinize them, ensuring fairness and preventing discriminatory outcomes.

3. **Avenues for Redress**: When AI-driven decisions go wrong, there must be clear avenues for redress. This means establishing impartial and accessible grievance mechanisms where individuals can challenge algorithmic decisions that unfairly impact them. Human overseers and independent review boards must be equipped to investigate complaints and hold those responsible for errors accountable.

4. **Public Scrutiny and Open-Source Development**: Secrecy breeds distrust. Governments deploying AI in governance must embrace transparency and public scrutiny. Open-sourcing algorithms and datasets where feasible fosters trust and allow independent researchers to identify and address potential biases. Public consultations and hackathons can further engage citizens in co-designing ethical frameworks and identifying potential unintended consequences.

5. **Continuous Learning and Adaptation**: The technological landscape is constantly evolving, and ethical frameworks must adapt with it. Ongoing research and development in responsible AI governance are crucial. Universities, technology companies, and civil society organizations must collaborate to develop best practices and share knowledge globally. Continuous learning and adaptation will ensure ethical frameworks remain relevant in the face of ever-evolving AI technology.

Ultimately, navigating the ethical minefield of AI in governance requires a multi-pronged approach. Robust frameworks, public engagement, and continuous learning are the cornerstones of ensuring AI serves the public good, enhances democracy, and fosters a more just and equitable society.

Impact on the Party System:

The Data-Driven Caucus: AI could reshape the power dynamics within political parties. With voter data and sentiment analysis readily available, party leadership could become more centralized, driven by algorithms suggesting strategies rather than grassroots movements. This shift could raise concerns about internal democracy and representation of diverse viewpoints. Imagine a scenario where party platforms are primarily shaped by AI-generated analyses of voter polls, potentially neglecting the voices of underrepresented communities or ignoring nuanced local concerns.
The Rise of the Technocrats: In an AI-powered governance landscape, expertise in data analysis and algorithm development could become increasingly influential. This could empower a new class of technocrats, blurring traditional party lines and potentially displacing established politicians. Imagine a scenario where experts in AI governance hold key positions in government, advising on policy decisions and wielding significant power based on their technical expertise rather than political experience.

The Reframing of the Debate: AI could usher in a new era of policy debates, where data-driven solutions and evidence-based reasoning take center stage. This could force traditional parties to adapt their platforms and policies, focusing on concrete outcomes and tangible results rather than purely ideological stances. Imagine a scenario where policy proposals are accompanied by AI simulations of their potential impact, allowing for more informed and nuanced discussions about their merits and drawbacks.

Current Applications and Possibilities:

While the full potential of AI in governance remains largely untapped, several pioneering initiatives offer glimpses of the future:

Estonia's X-Road system: This secure online platform allows citizens to access government services seamlessly, from filing taxes to applying for permits, making Estonian governance remarkably efficient and transparent.

Taiwan's "Justify AI" project: This initiative is developing AI tools to automate legal research and provide judges with relevant precedents, aiming to improve the efficiency and consistency of judicial decisions.

Canada's pilot project using AI for risk assessment in criminal justice: This project seeks to develop an AI tool that could predict recidivism risk with greater accuracy and reduce racial bias in sentencing decisions.

These examples showcase the potential of AI to streamline processes, enhance decision-making, and promote transparency in governance. However, they also highlight the critical need for robust ethical frameworks, citizen oversight, and continuous monitoring to mitigate potential biases and ensure AI serves the public good.

Conclusion: A Human-Machine Tango on the Political Stage:

The rise of AI in governance presents a complex and multifaceted challenge. It offers an incredible array of potential benefits, from increased efficiency and citizen engagement to evidence-based policymaking. However, alongside these promises lie substantial risks: concerns about algorithmic bias, erosion of trust, and the potential for AI to become a tool for oppression or manipulation. Ultimately, the future of AI in governance depends on our ability to navigate this ethical minefield with caution, clarity, and a deep commitment to democratic principles. It is a human-machine tango where, with careful choreography and shared responsibility, the outcome can be a more responsive, informed, and equitable political landscape for all.

Chapter 13: Navigating the American Trilemma: A Republic Forged in Democratic Ideals.

The American political landscape presents a unique and often paradoxical trilemma. We are a nation that yearns for both individual liberty and collective progress, fueled by the fire of democratic ideals yet constrained by the framework of a constitutional republic. This tension, this dance between freedom and responsibility, shapes every facet of our political discourse and every challenge we face.

It is easy to fall into pessimism, to lament the partisan gridlock, the social divisions, and the seemingly intractable problems that plague our national dialogue. But to abandon hope is to surrender to the echoes of the trilemma, to allow them to drown out the chorus of a better tomorrow. Instead, we must remember that America was not born of resignation, but of revolution.

Our nation's foundations lie not just in the democratic aspirations espoused in the Declaration of Independence, but also in the sober pragmatism embedded within the Constitution. These two pillars, democracy and republic, are not at odds, but rather two sides of the same coin. Democracy provides the engine, the fuel for our aspirations, while the republic offers the guardrails, the framework that ensures individual rights are protected and progress is pursued responsibly.

Therefore, navigating the American trilemma requires a multi-pronged approach, a symphony of action played on the instruments of both engagement and restraint.

The Imperative of Informed Citizens:

Firstly, we must be a nation of informed citizens, not passive spectators. Casting a ballot is not a mere ritual, but a responsibility. We must delve beyond the soundbites and headlines, scrutinize information from diverse sources, and hold our elected officials accountable for their actions. Knowledge is not just power; it is the bedrock of a functioning democracy.

Finding Common Ground Amidst Division:

Secondly, we must acknowledge and grapple with our divisions. Social media echo chambers and partisan narratives make it tempting to demonize those who hold different views. But progress cannot be forged in silos. We must bridge the divides, engage in respectful dialogue, and seek common ground where possible. Remember, the American story is one of bridges built, not walls erected.

Empowering Third-Party Movements:

Thirdly, we must recognize that the two-party system, while deeply entrenched, is not an immutable force. Third-party movements and independent voices offer fresh perspectives and potential alternatives. Supporting, and even participating in, their efforts can inject new ideas into the political discourse and challenge the status quo.

Reimagining Democracy:

Fourthly, we must embrace the need to constantly refine and improve our democratic practices. This may involve exploring alternative voting systems, promoting civic education from a young age, and fostering open dialogue across ideological divides. A democracy that stagnates is a democracy that dies.

Holding the Flame of Hope:

Finally, we must never lose sight of hope. Remember, hope is not a passive sentiment; it is a flame that must be actively nurtured. Every informed vote cast, every act of civic engagement, every voice raised in dissent against injustice fuels this flame. Let us embrace the challenge, not with pessimism, but with the understanding that the power to shape our future lies not in the hands of a few, but in the collective voice of the American people. Together, we can build a more just, fair, and vibrant democracy, one where the echoes of the trilemma fade into a distant memory, replaced by the harmonious chorus of a nation united in its pursuit of a better tomorrow.

The End